Preface

We are not really sure when we decided to complete a second photo-prose book. We just knew that after we completed our first book, *Paperback Tears: The Journey Begins Now (2011),* that there would eventually be a second book. We have been friends for 50 years and we have lived hundreds of miles apart for about 40 years. We have not had the luxury of visiting one and other, even on a semi-regular basis. Despite this, we have been lifelong friends who think about each other daily and continue to love one and other regardless of whether we see each other or not.

Cathleen Jo Faruque is a literary poet and Amy Folse is a visual poet. Our work is in part presented in this book. It is uniquely our own and serves as a reflection of our passion for life. It means a great deal to both of us, we hope it carries meaning for you!

Alone

Cathleen Jo Faruque ©

My heart pulsates your name
desire lost in the stroke of a beat
A nomadic, errant soul
mislaid torment retentions of you
simply propitious in nearness to you.
Can the forsaken endure?
or will provocation end new?
Days pass extended and forlorn
without you here.
Days pass in minutes
Minutes pass in years
Waiting for
hoping for
Longing for
You.

Publisher: Createspace Independent Publishing Platform, 410 Terry Avenue North, Seattle, WA 98109-5210 USA

6" x 9" (15.24 x 22.86 cm) Full Color on White paper

ISBN-13: 978-1505710762 (CreateSpace-Assigned)
ISBN-10: 1505710766

Acknowledgement

If most of us were to write a book on life, the first 500 or so pages would be acknowledgements because we do not exist for ourselves. We are all mere reflections of one and other. This is our second book of photo-prose, and we honestly cannot think of a single person to acknowledge. Probably because no singular person or even multiple persons serve as a key influence. Hence, we wish to acknowledge every one we know, living or dead, real or imagined, that made this book a reality.

Dedication

This book is dedicated to the planet Earth. We are proud children of the Mother Earth and do our best to contribute to her long and healthy life. Over a half a century ago, we became daughters of Mother Earth. She gifted us our Earthly Name: Kickapoo Skump.

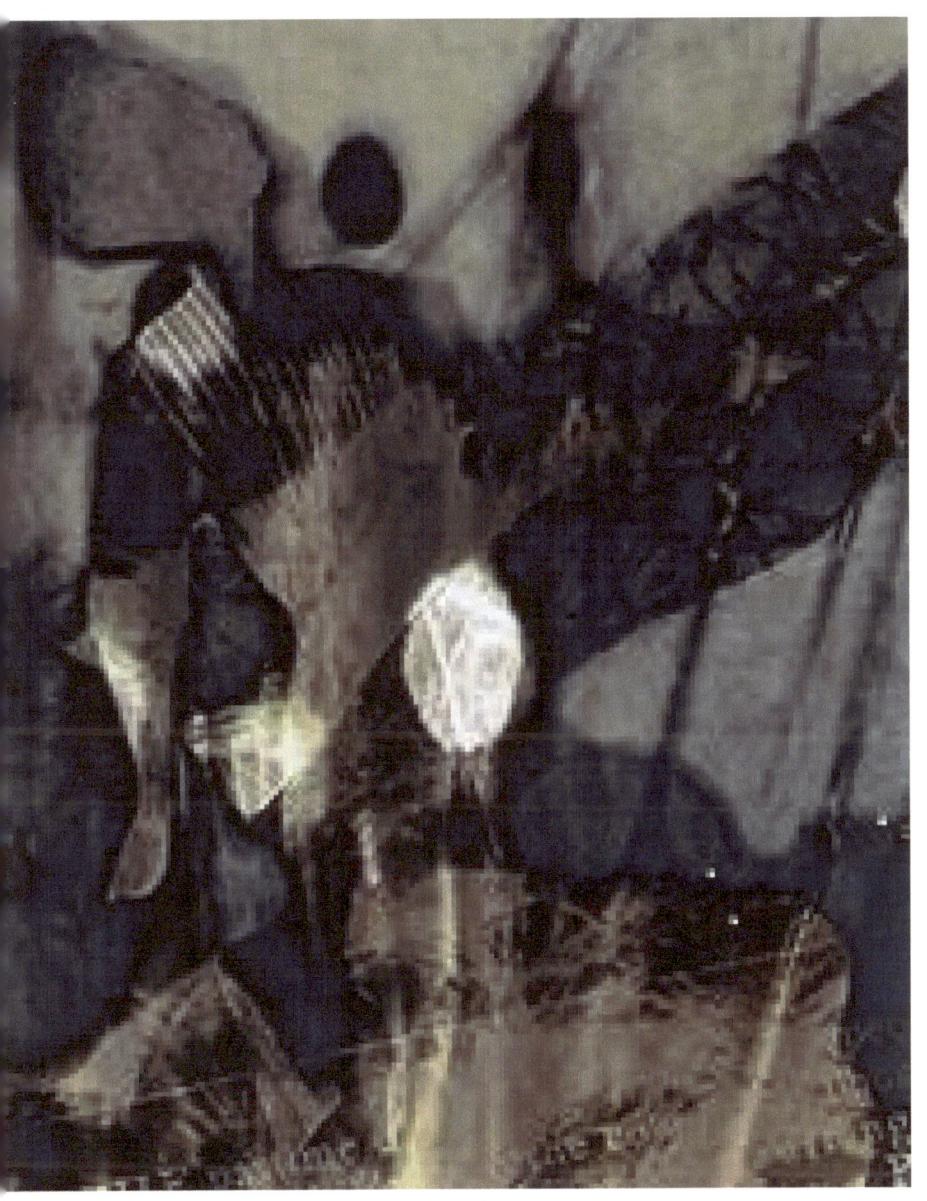

Apartment Living

Cathleen Jo Faruque ©

Images
Of a cracked
Window.
Small space
Dirty place.
Panes of glass
Like shards
In boxes
Of wood,
Brick,
Steel,
Concrete.

Images on a
Window.
White
Upon
White,
Glaring
Blurs,
Masked
Shadows,
Figurines,
Congregate,
Dancing
Images on
A window.

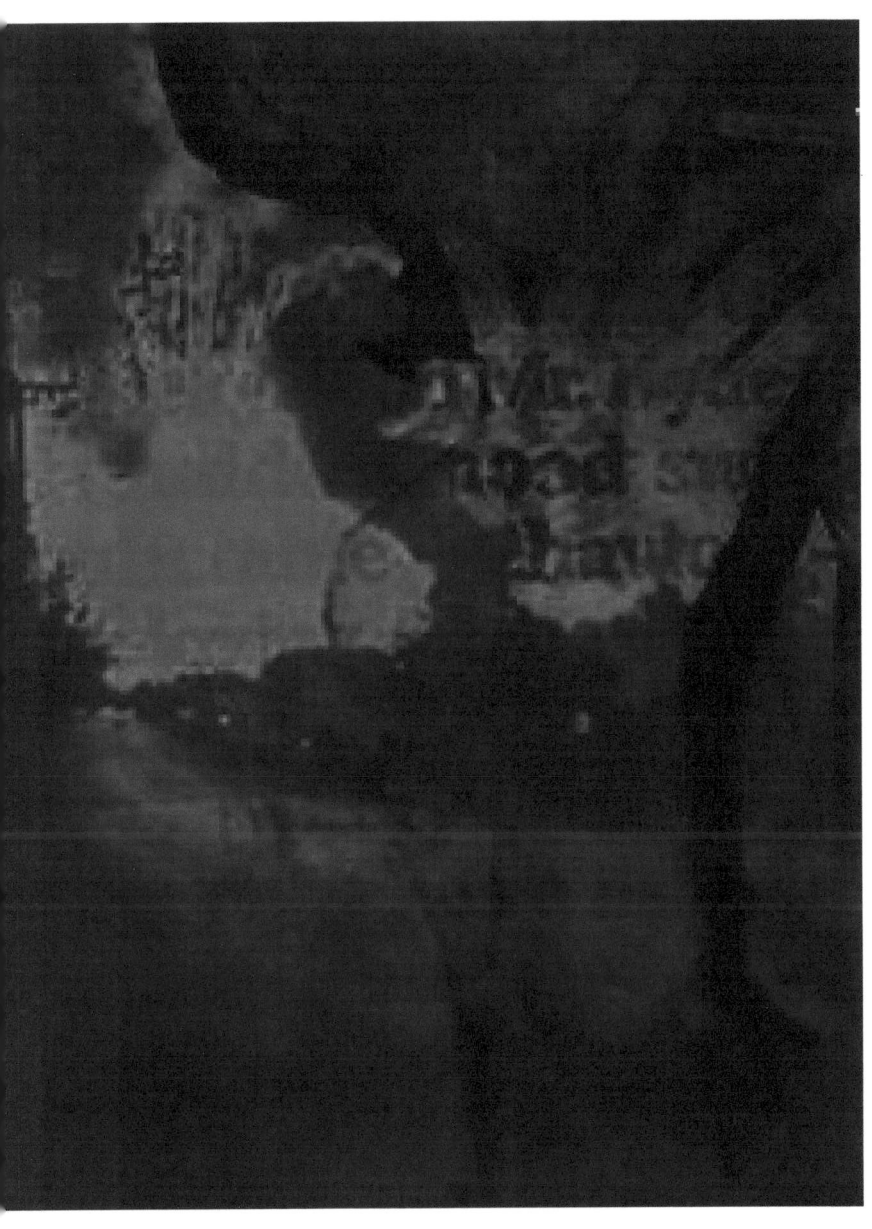

Breathing

Cathleen Jo Faruque ©

Breathing
Slowly heart beat
Increased
By thoughts of you
Embraced in
Memory.
Time is a
Wicked game.
Memories and
Agony for
A tormented soul
Searching for you.
Lost by wicked
Time
Iniquitous memories
Desires
Yearning
Desires.
Gone astray by time
Captured in this body
Imprisoned in this heart
Tortured in this mind
Tormented in this soul.

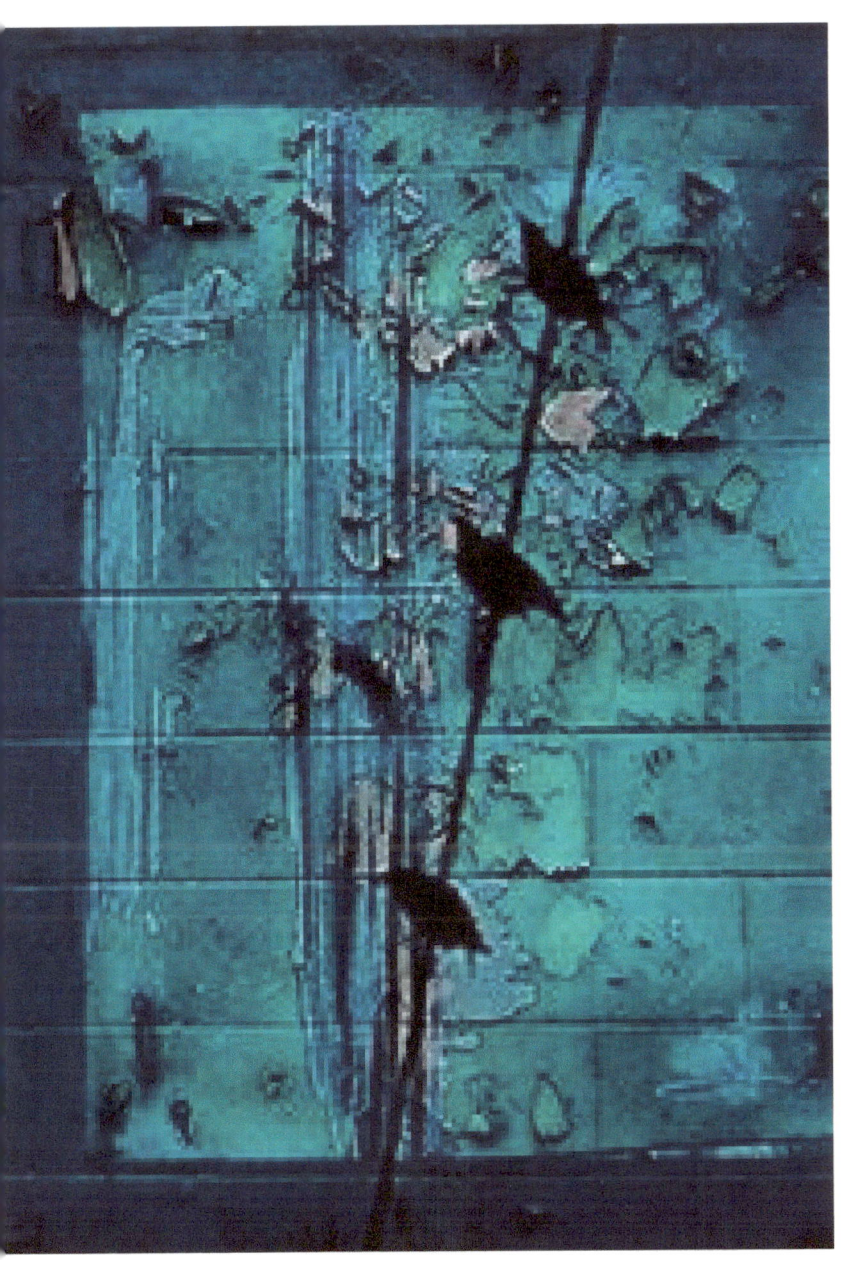

© Amy Folse

Cold Hard Rain

Cathleen Jo Faruque ©

I listen to the sounds of the rain
outside my window
bitter
sweetly cold
paced rhythms
blue on blue
iced solitude.
Like my heart
cold as ice
on a wintery
day.
No reprieve
No answer
No reason
Only silence in
bitter
sweetly cold
blue on blue
rain.
October rains
chill to the bone
like my heart
chilled to the
core.
Little hope for thaw
perhaps
when spring comes.

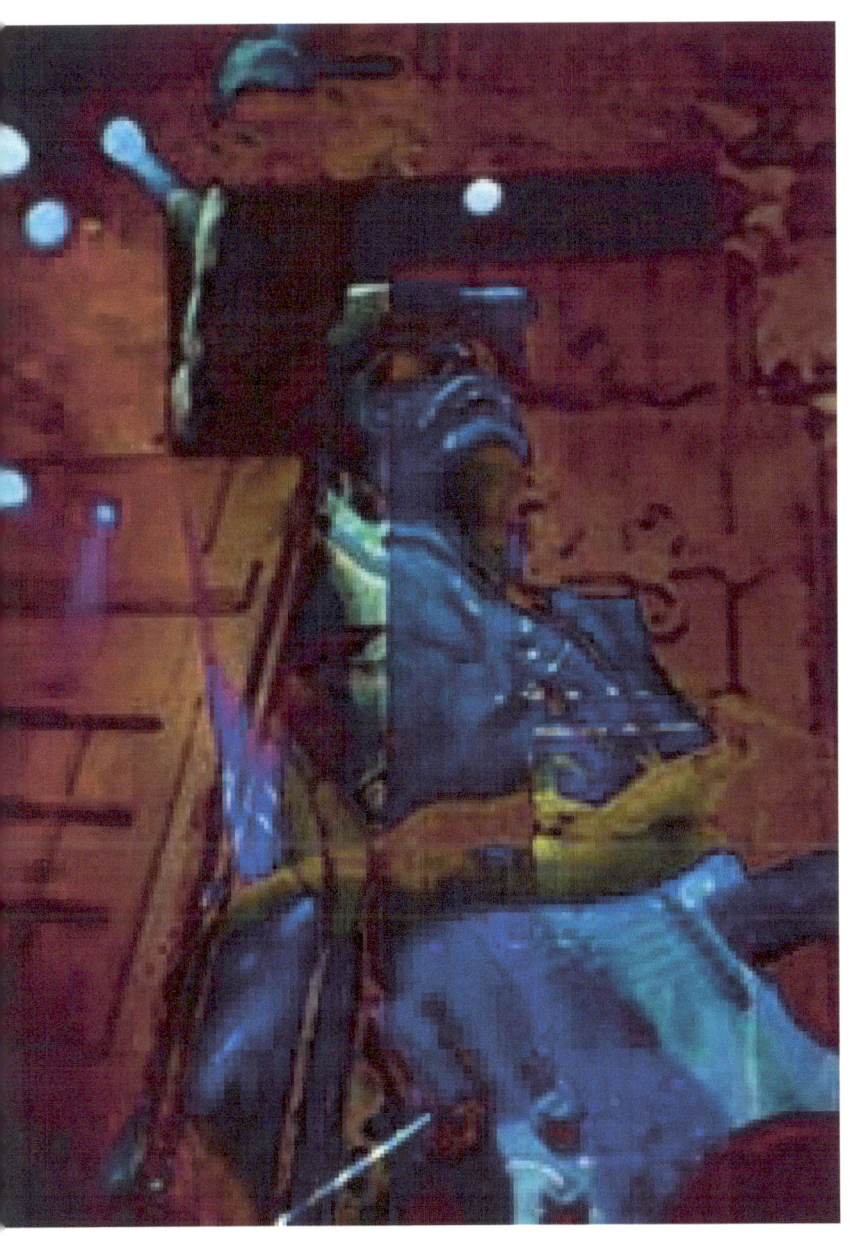

© Amy Folse

Fallen

Cathleen Jo Faruque ©

Black is the sky
Distinguishing crisp unadorned stars
No twinkle, no flash
Just scattered and flawless
Rotund points of white
Ashen moon face shines
Between barren quiescent trees
Caustic stench of rotting leaves
Create an eerie setting
To a sleepless autumn night
Silence intervallic by a
Black cat prepared to ambush
Heckling the small quarry
That takes off in the night.
Ears disgruntled by the intrusion
Of tranquility gone astray
And the affable thoughts
Of a friend who is so ever far away.

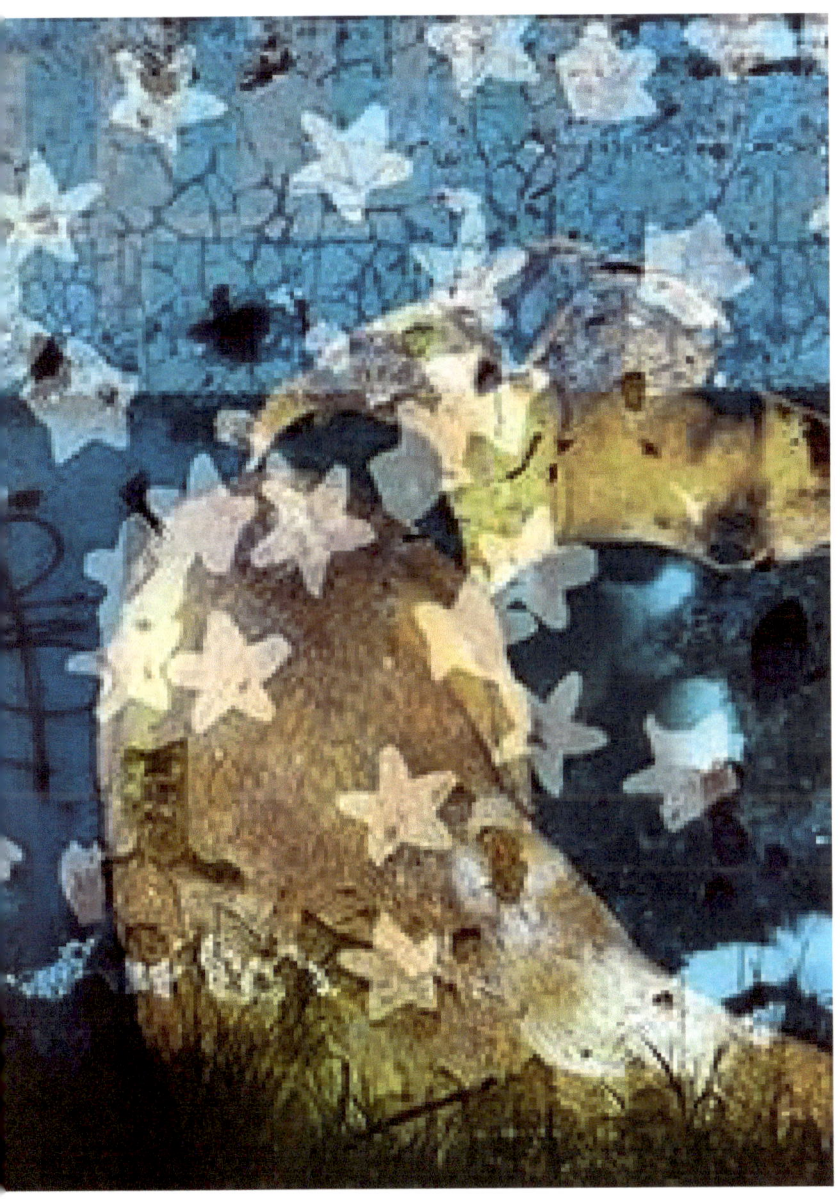

© Amy Folse

Forget About Me

Cathleen Jo Faruque ©

Runoff devotion

Dead on

Proscribe excess

Absolve yourself

All about you

All about you

Lost heart

Convivial repast

Continual omission

Possibly,

Perhaps not

Forget yourself

Overlook me

I don't need this

I don't want this

All about you

All about you.

Overflow devotion

So erroneous

So poignant

Forget

Forgive

Maybe you should

Forget me.

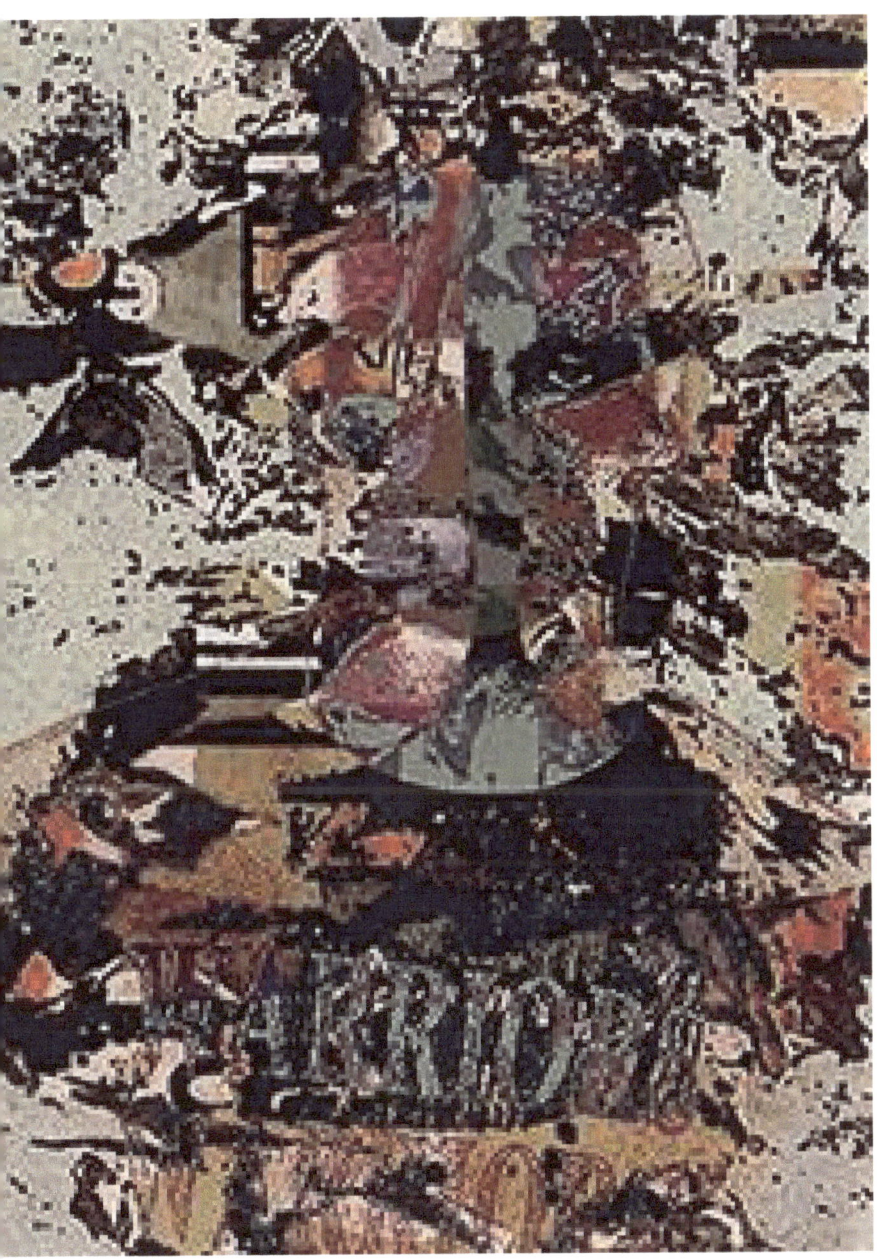

© Amy Folse

Gimme a Minute

Cathleen Jo Faruque ©

Changes fill the body
No stopping it
Once clear mirrors
Now haze over glassy-eyed
Days that merge
Converge
Pass quickly
Where did the day go?
Hell with that!
Where did the year go?
Gliding to base
Foundation slants
Windows claim years of dirt
Tears belong to youth
My heart is a child
But the seasons pass
I don't know
Fear of change
But changes fill my soul
Waiting for you
That was long ago
Hesitating
Built a life in hope of you
But hope is for the young

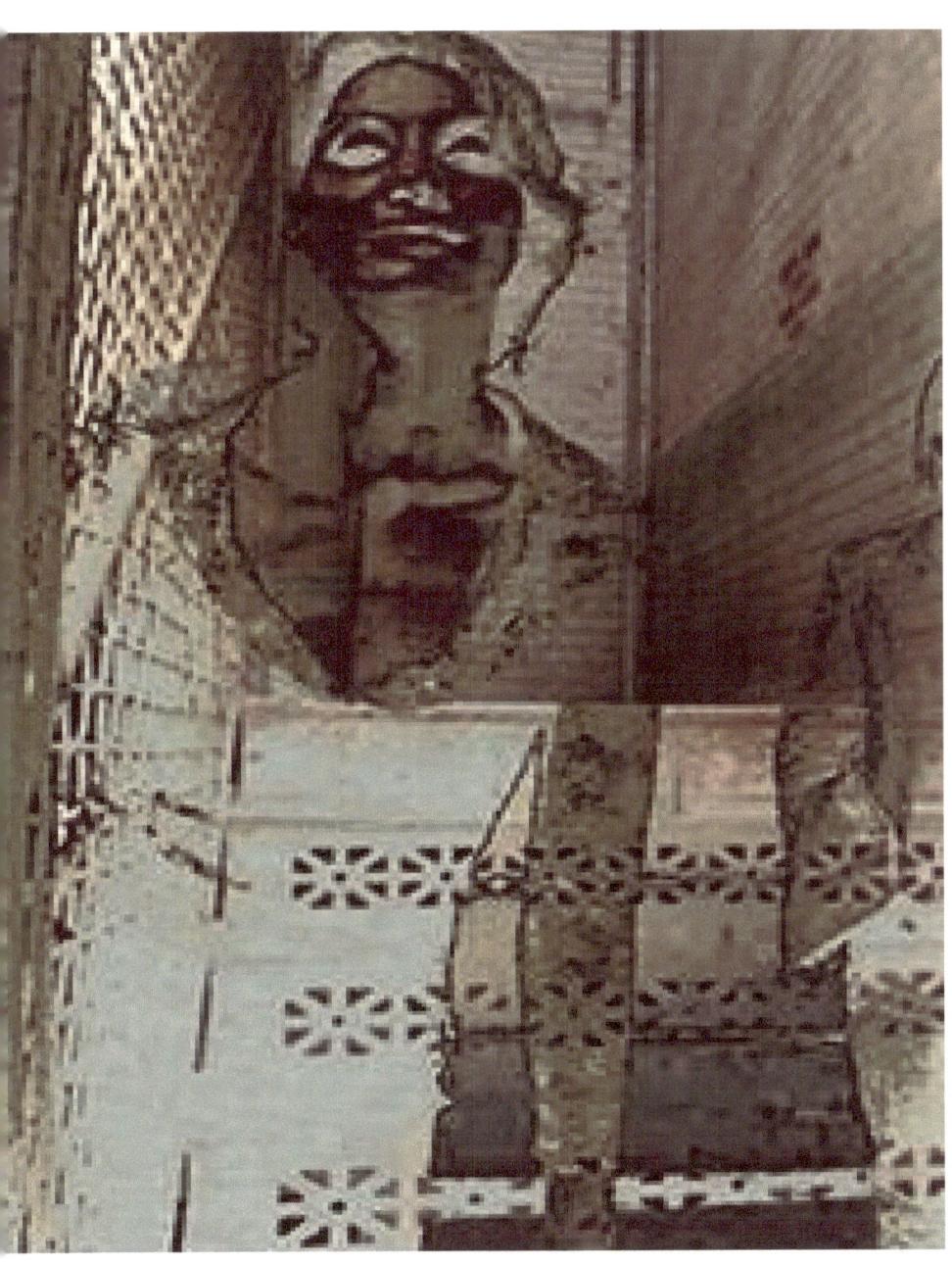

Heart of Stone

Cathleen Jo Faruque ©

Flutters feathery

Ice torrents on

Cascade eyes

Blinded by hindsight

Caressed blue lips

Fallen side glances

Distant stabs

Shiny blades

Of fire storm

Crescendos crash

Foam milk waves.

Heart of stone

Dispersed memories

Catapulting shame

Nowhere to turn

Nowhere to turn

Just hate you.

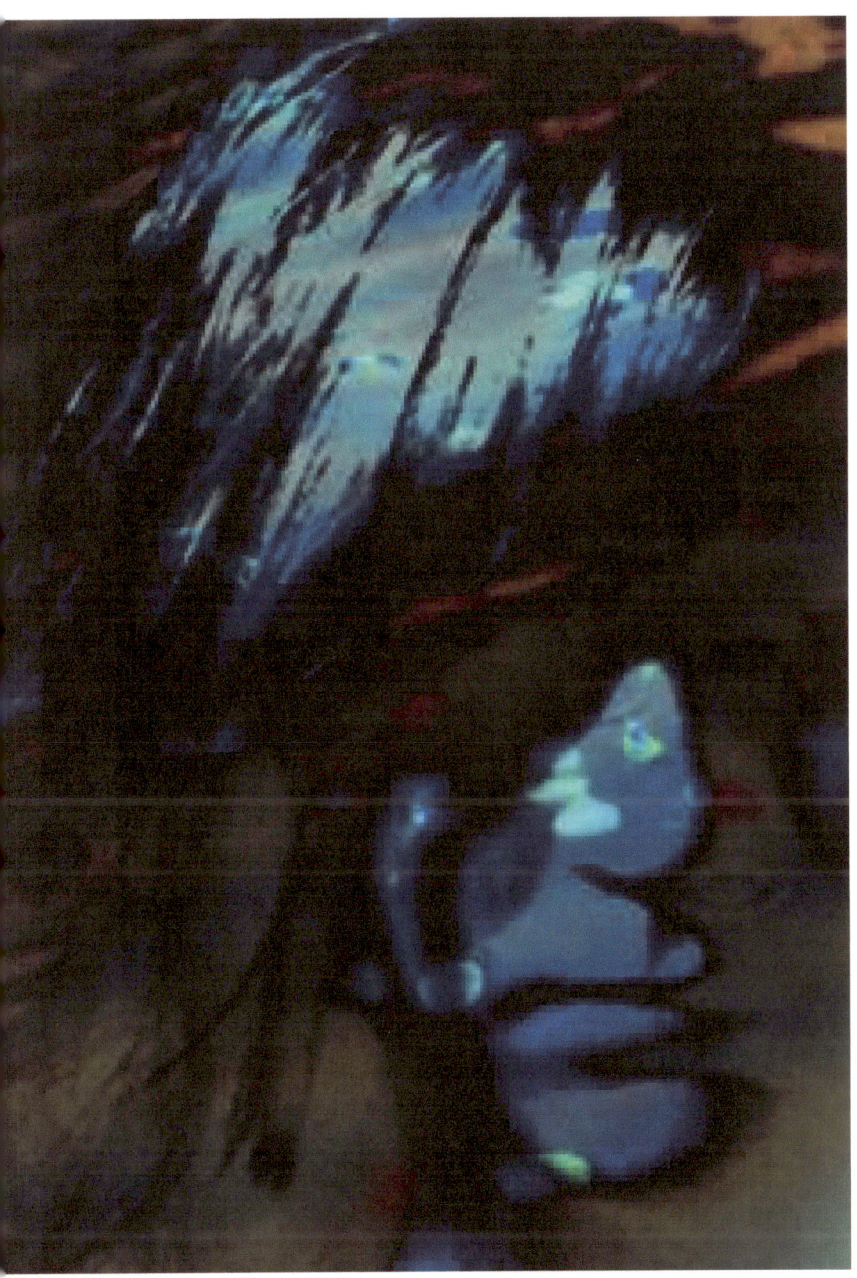

Grey Heart

Cathleen Jo Faruque ©

Reaching through the darkness
I love you, Love you more than I can say
Time spirals descends another day
Somewhere reaching for night
Need you to feel me

Reaching you through the darkness
To hold you through the darkened sky
But you love someone more than I
In the yawning night of dawn
Need you near to me

Reaching through the darkness
I love you, Love you, more than I can say
Even when your heart turned away
Expended day thinking of you
Wish you would receive me

Reaching through the darkness
Your hand slips through mine
Distance floats with time beyond
Restricted corners of my mind
You are near me

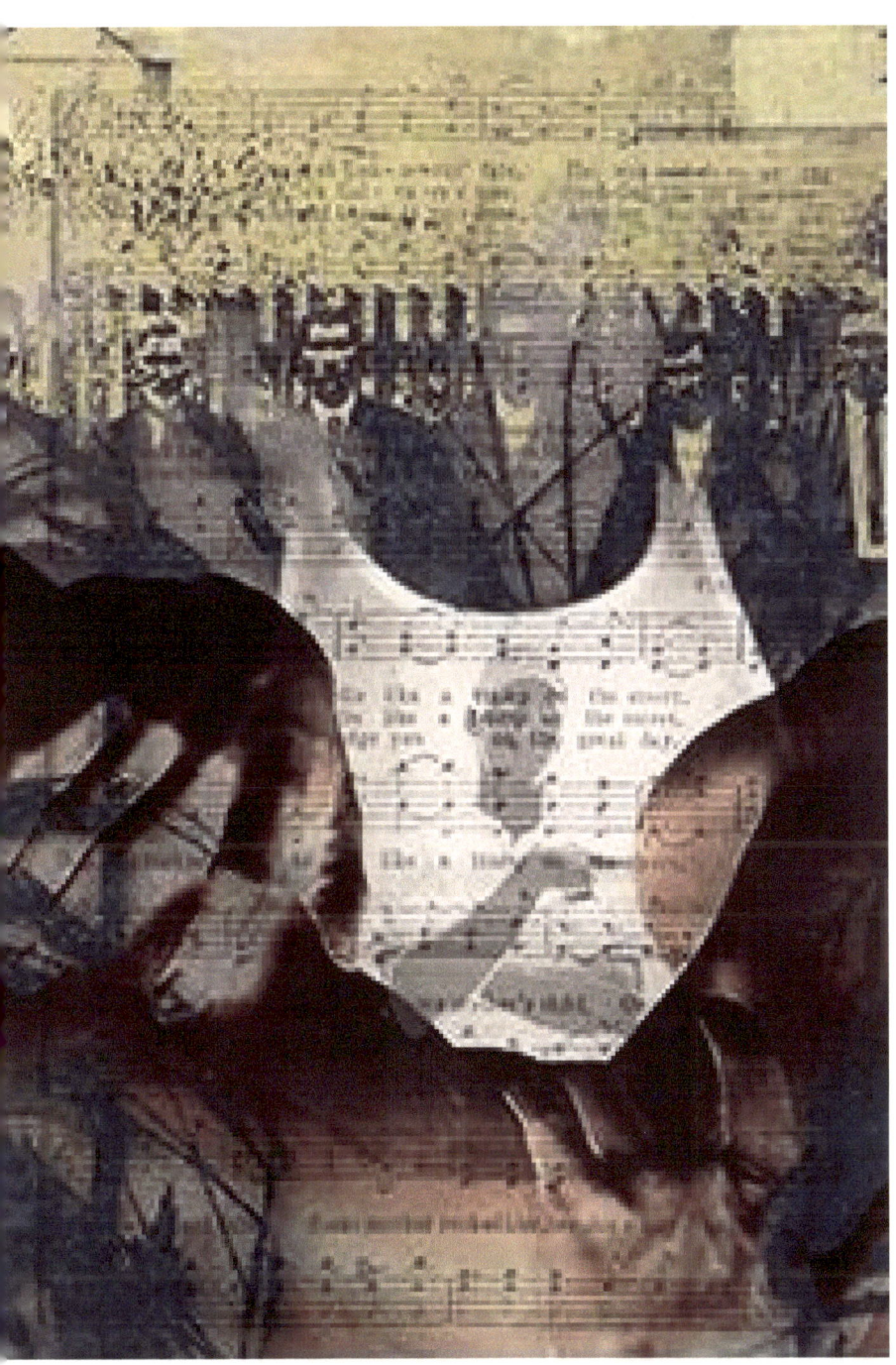

Home

Cathleen Jo Faruque ©

Sweet breathe
Missed.
Kiss of
Freedom.

Selective features,
White expanses,
Fading apples,
Dying leaves,
Icy winds.

Whipped up
Like perfume to
Plum red faces.

Your arms
Unfold
And
You are
Home.

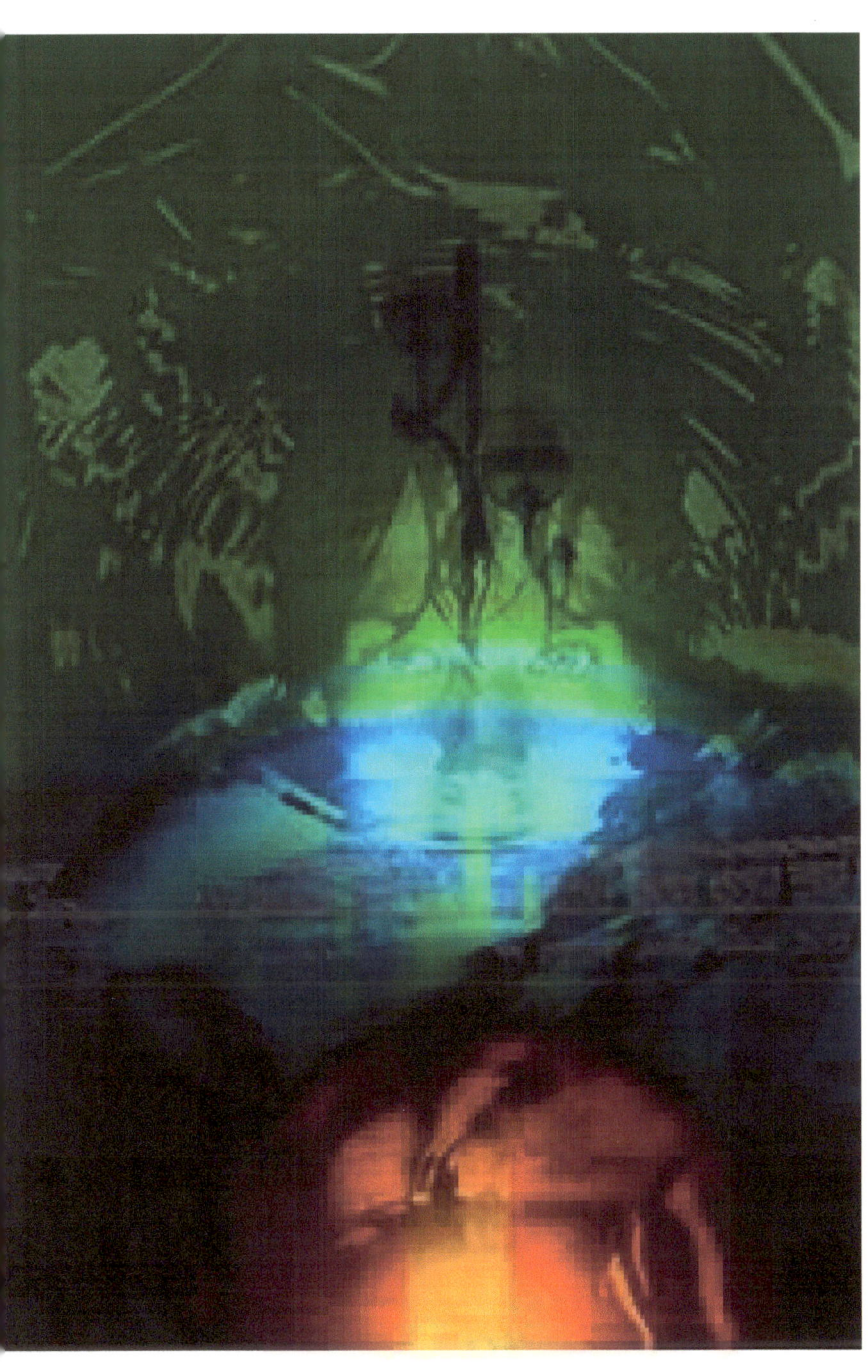

Ice Moon

Cathleen Jo Faruque ©

Ice Moon connect and touch
Cold and unattainable reach
Triumphantly glow to Earth in
Sweet perigee
Making the brilliant sphere
Bigger, brighter, perpetual
Dancing in the black liquid sky.
Dreaming of the distance
From the Ice Moon to
Your heart.
Hanging on to the night
When your touch converges
And is attainable on this
Icy winter night.
Clandestine moments that transpire
An Ice Moon and transparent breath.
Draw near to welcome me
You are the Ice Moon.
Be as attainable as the limits of
Universe and time.
Conceal not your secrets
But share your wispy light
Cast a glow over the frozen
Wasteland of lake and trees.
Embrace the stars in the wintery sky.
Tangle in the night with
Venus and Mars.
Be not overshadowed by eclipse,
Cloud, rain, or snow.
Share the mysteries of this icy night
And hold me in your gentle embrace.

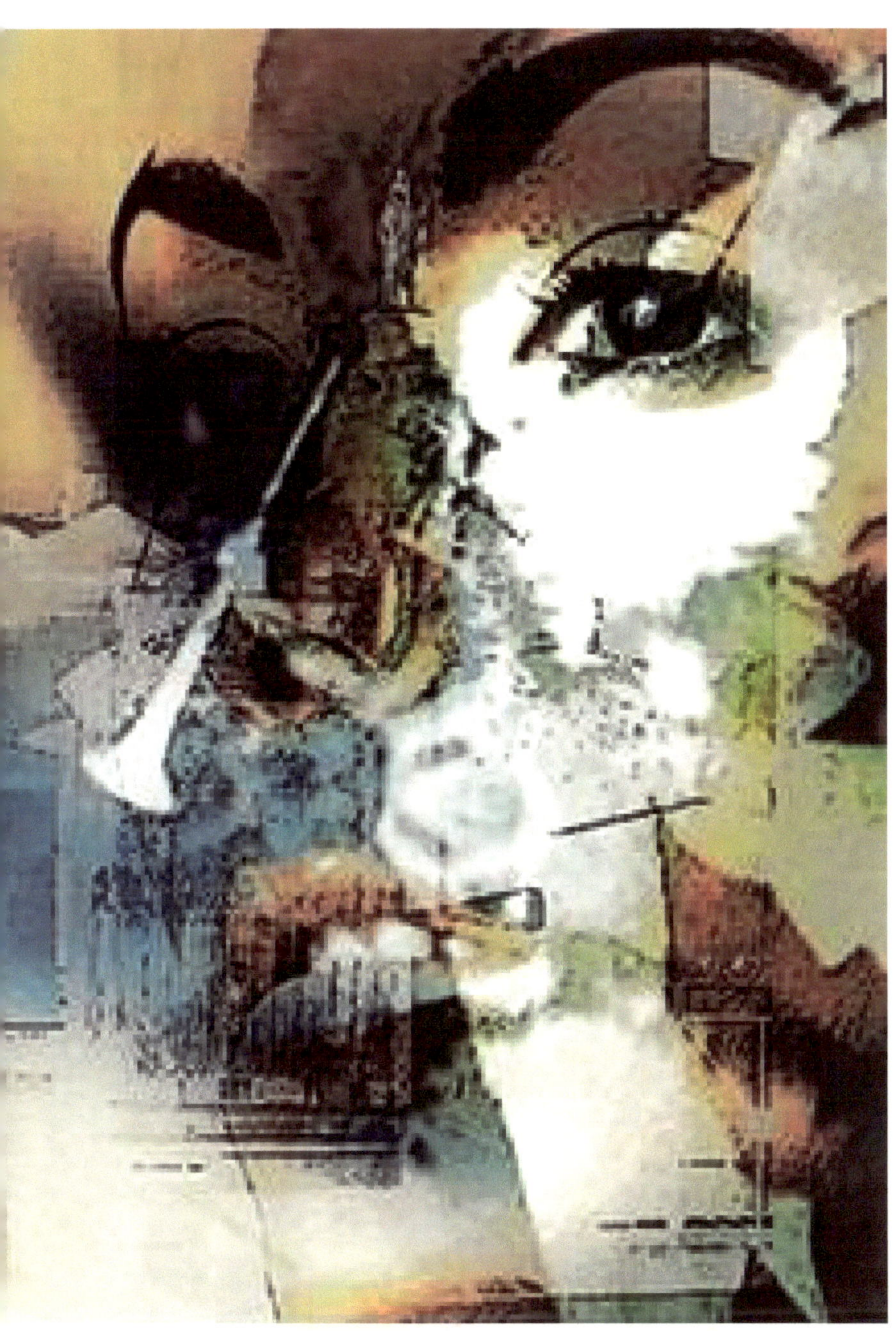

© Amy Folse

Infinite

Cathleen Jo Faruque ©

Like a infinite small repast

The harshest of looking glass

A fragment lost in one's time

Recaptured through precarious thought.

I know you are there inside

But I don't wish to be cast aside

I see the way you cast your glance

And look at her with milk soft smile.

Lips so beautiful never to be mine

My heart washed in yours entwined

How days pass into weeks

Soon to be passed by with regret.

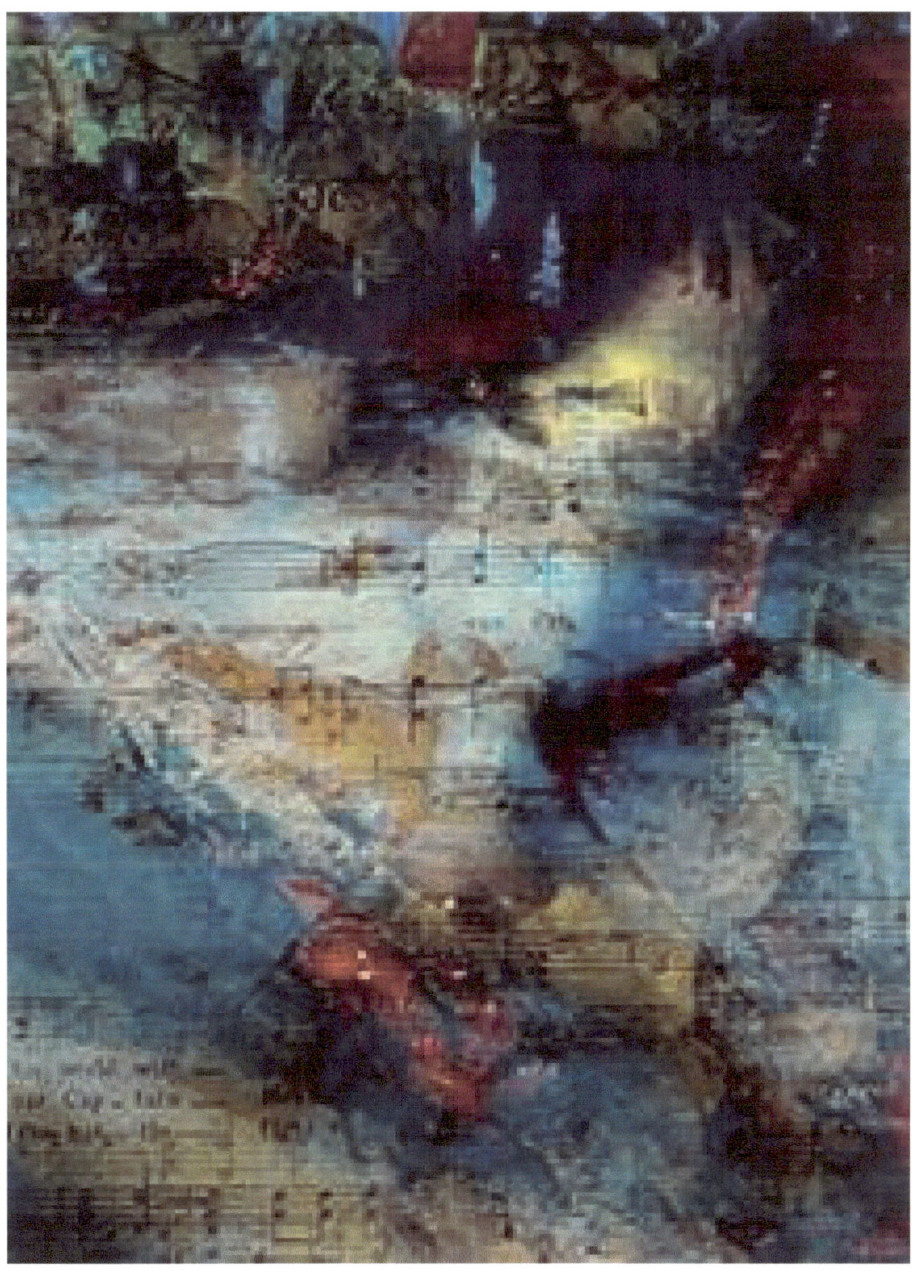

© Amy Folse

Lonely Night

Cathleen Jo Faruque ©

Half-moon casting shimmering
Glows through hazy clouds
Stars shining brightly on a summer evening
A lone plane passes in slow descent.
I wish to be on that plane
But it doesn't go to the place I need to be.
It merely is a symbol
A memory of travel once made
Time lost
Gazing in the cool evening sky
Makes me wonder
Where you are now
A day of bright bursting sunshine
High heat
Humidity
Chance of rain with little doubt
For it is the rainy season now
Or so I have been told.
Seems the dry spell makes it
All so unreal in its own way.
A path that leads to only daydreams
Possibilities
What if
what if
what if?
But there is only now
There is only here
There is only this
Lonely night.

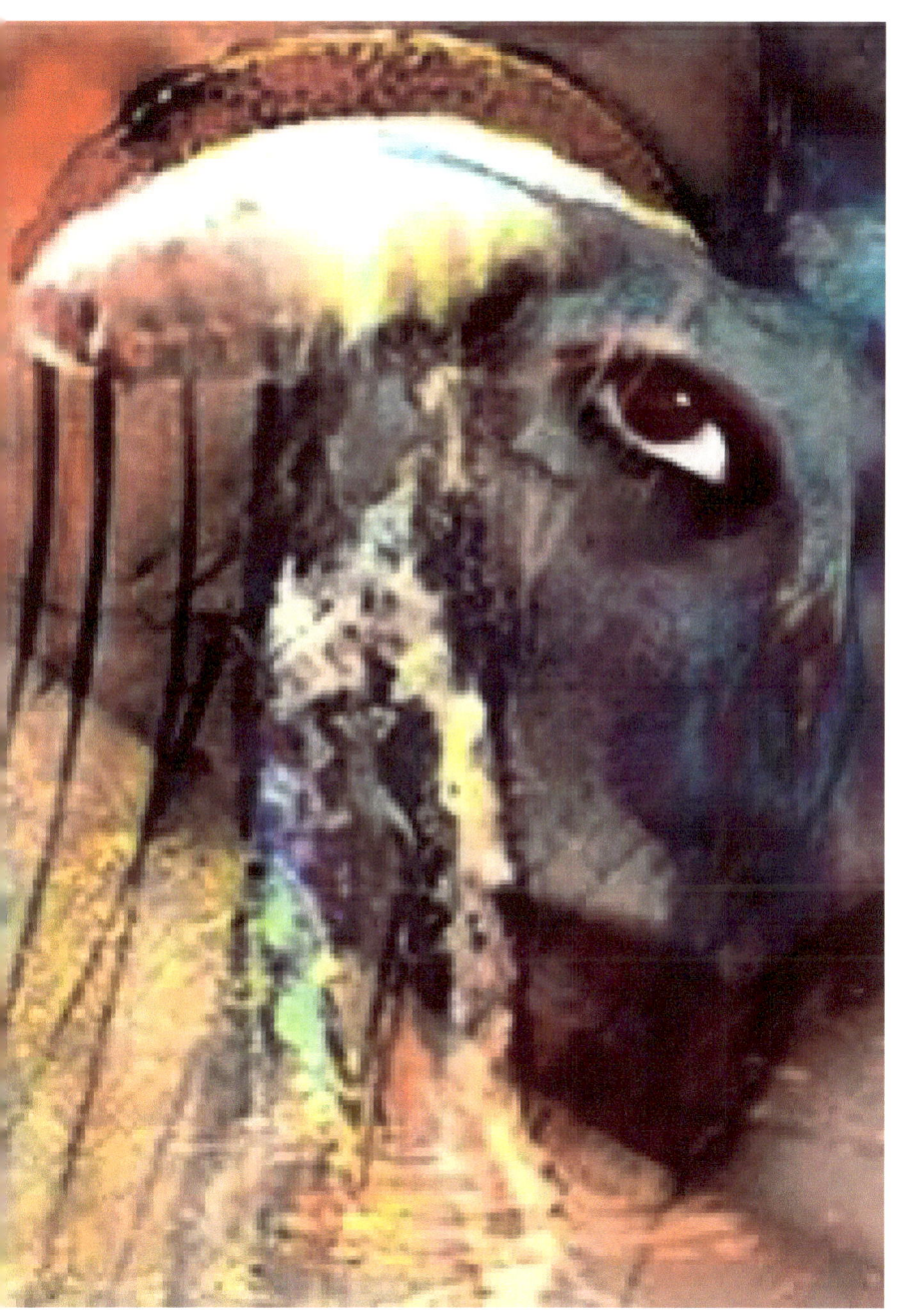

© Amy Folse

Malicious Intent

Cathleen Jo Faruque ©

When you know his mutilation

Abjuration

The mendacity incinerates

Duplicity

To ashes the torment

Deceit

The bane of subsistence

Inveterate

Chasm to the soul

Inconceivable

Entrenched obscured

Malevolent clandestine

Abhorrence incinerates

Nothingness is preferable

To perfidy

Of one you love

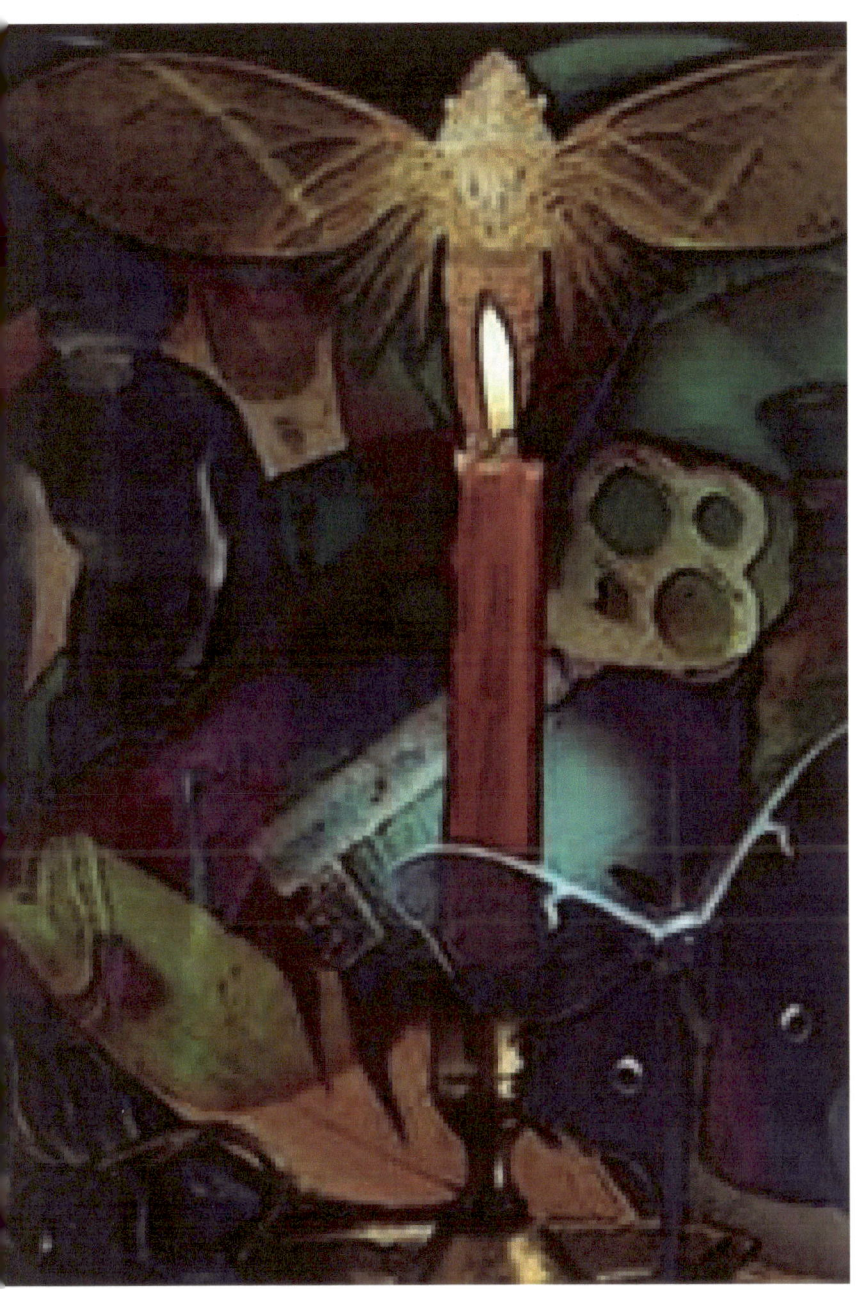

© Amy Folse

Memories of Minnesota

Cathleen Jo Faruque ©

Don't really know
Anymore.

Far,
Fuzzy,
Silent
Picture.

Cold,
White,
Crystals
Form
Blue
Ice.
Fading
Twilight.

Lasting
Memory.

One tear
One misery

Daybreak
Cool,
Lacking
Motion.

Just a
Memory.

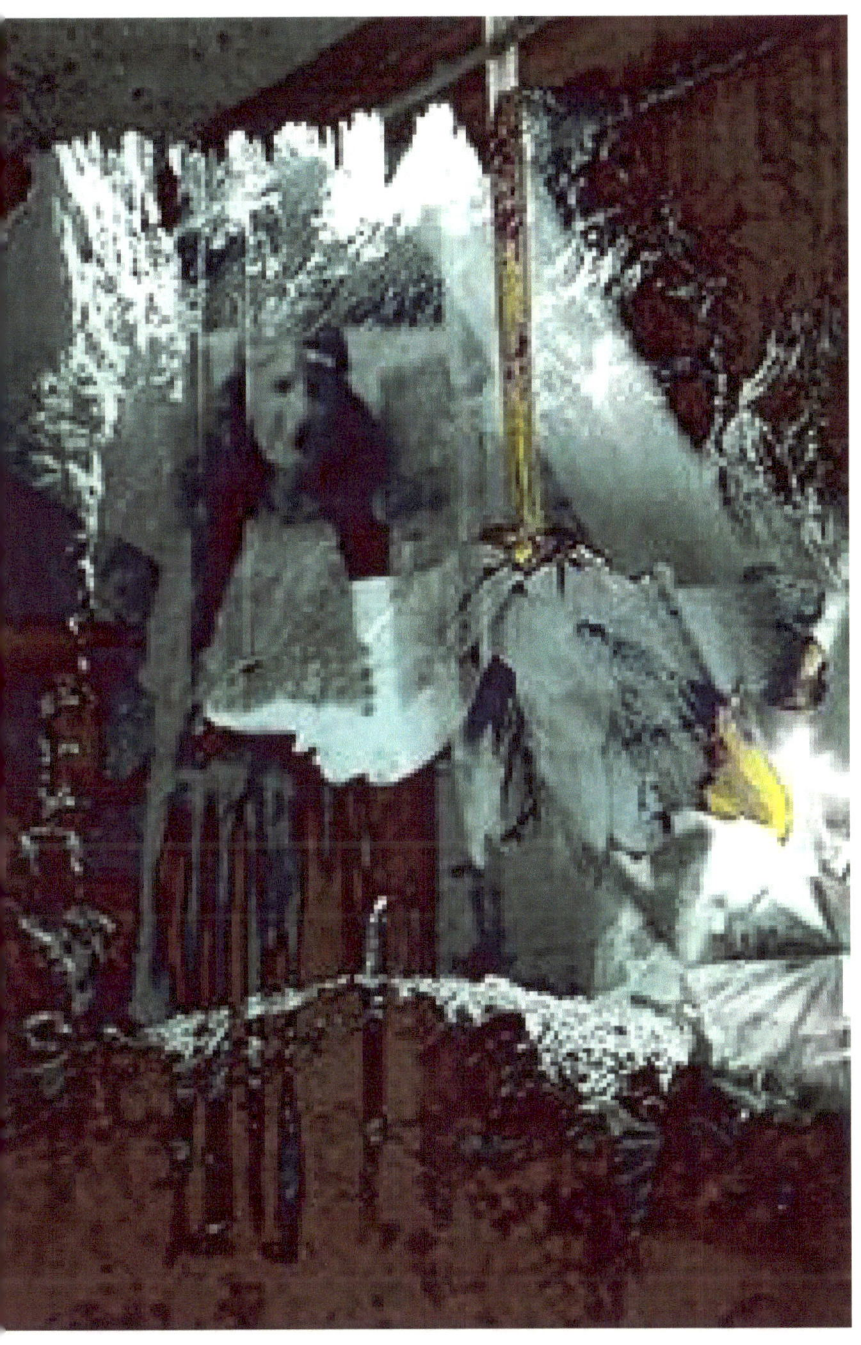

© Amy Folse

Memories of You

Cathleen Jo Faruque ©

Vivid night sky
Star beams diminish to golden obscure moon
Chilled winter winds
Blister to the bone
Shawl wrapped securely
Hands in pockets
Head turned down
Sprint to interior hospitality.
Recollections of you
Unconsciously they come
Of the day buoyant by sun and moon
Waters pale against hazy blue skies
Restful sway of a dinghy
Fleeting and without concern
Seagulls float against water's surf
Shawl wrapped cozily
Arms extended
High spirited hearts elevated
Canopy lunges outward
Providence fulfilled
Quest understood
Memories of you.

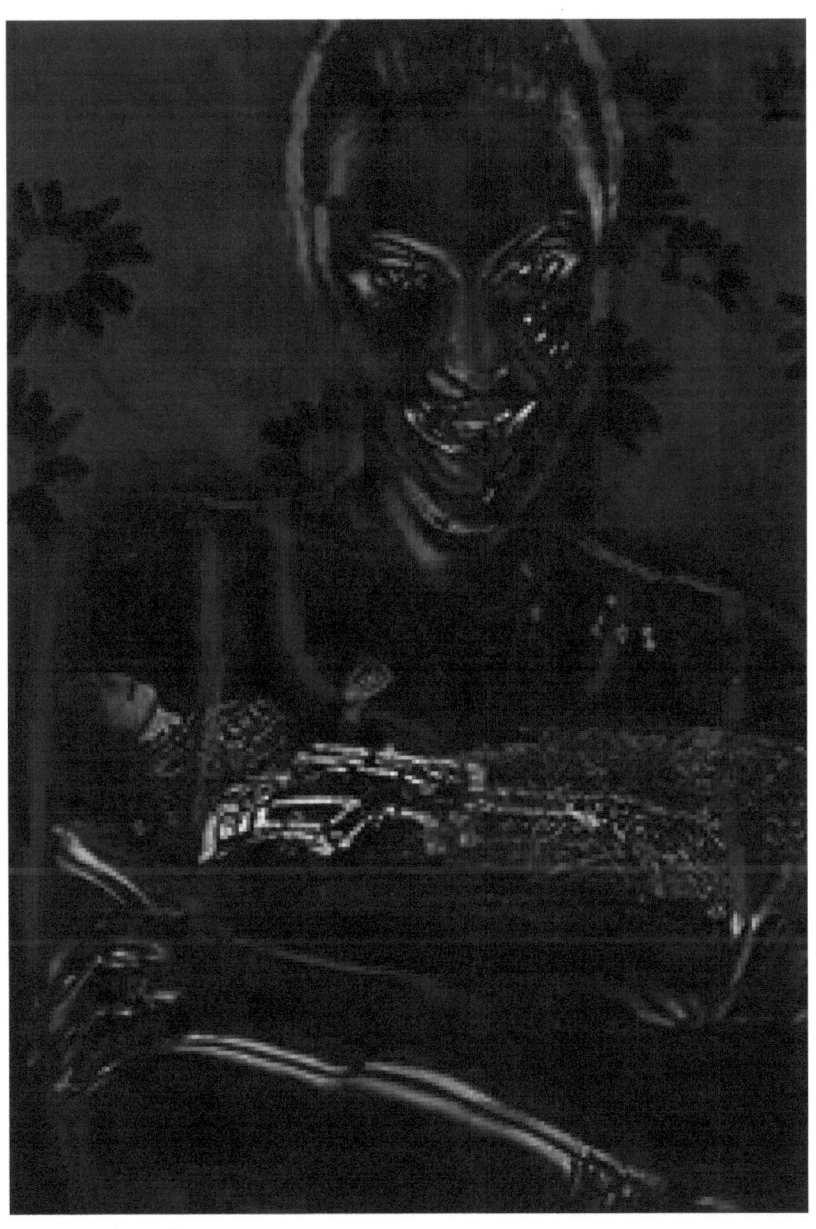

© Amy Folse

Mortality

Cathleen Jo Faruque ©

Laughing
In a
Blanket
Of white
Rain.
Crying on
Protruding
Black
Skies.
Swimming
In a sea
Of golden
Dirt.
Drowning...
Death
Comes slowly.

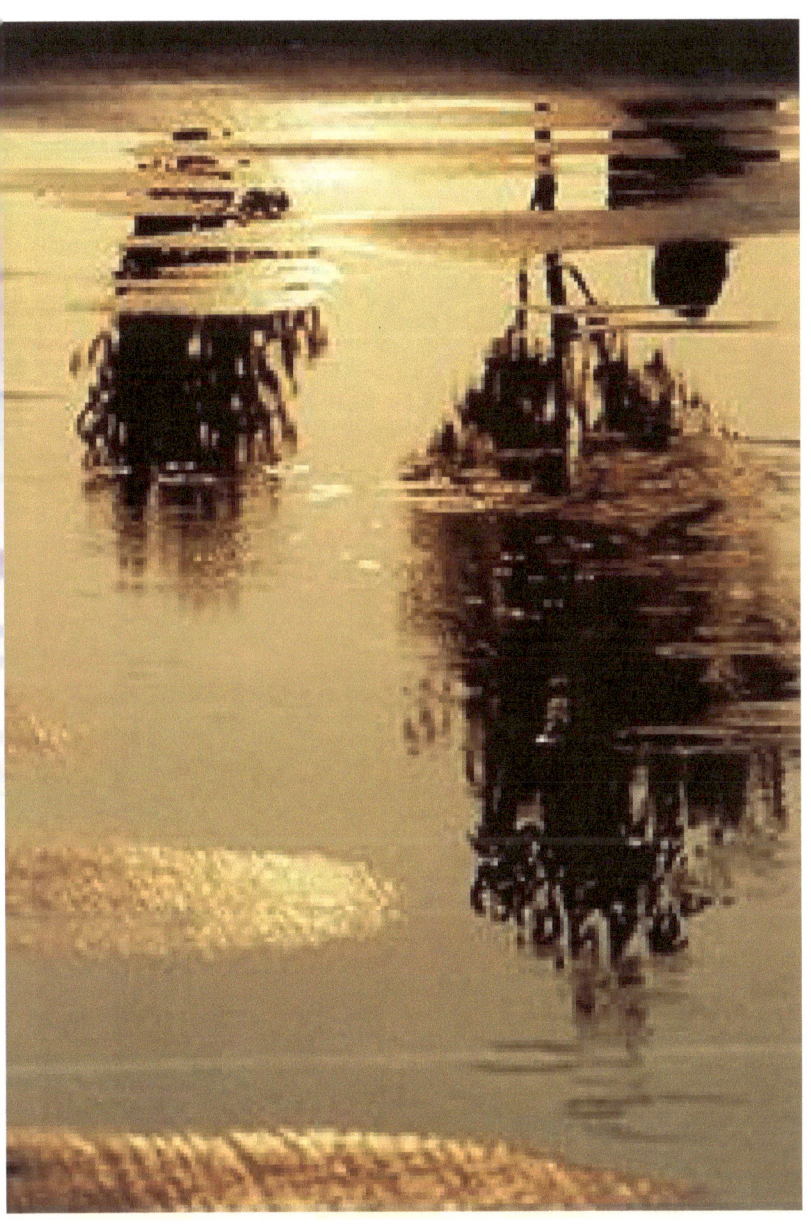

© Amy Folse

Never Tells

Cathleen Jo Faruque ©

I met
You discreetly.
Promised
Secrecy.
Oh I wish
Quite
Openly.

I love you,
I love you!
I have not
Told you,
I won't tell you
Not Yet.

I smiled
You frowned
I pulled
You pushed.
Left me
Please
Not
Yet.

Fears
For tears
Flow
Freely
Indiscrete

I love you,
I love you!
But I can't tell you
I won't
I never will.

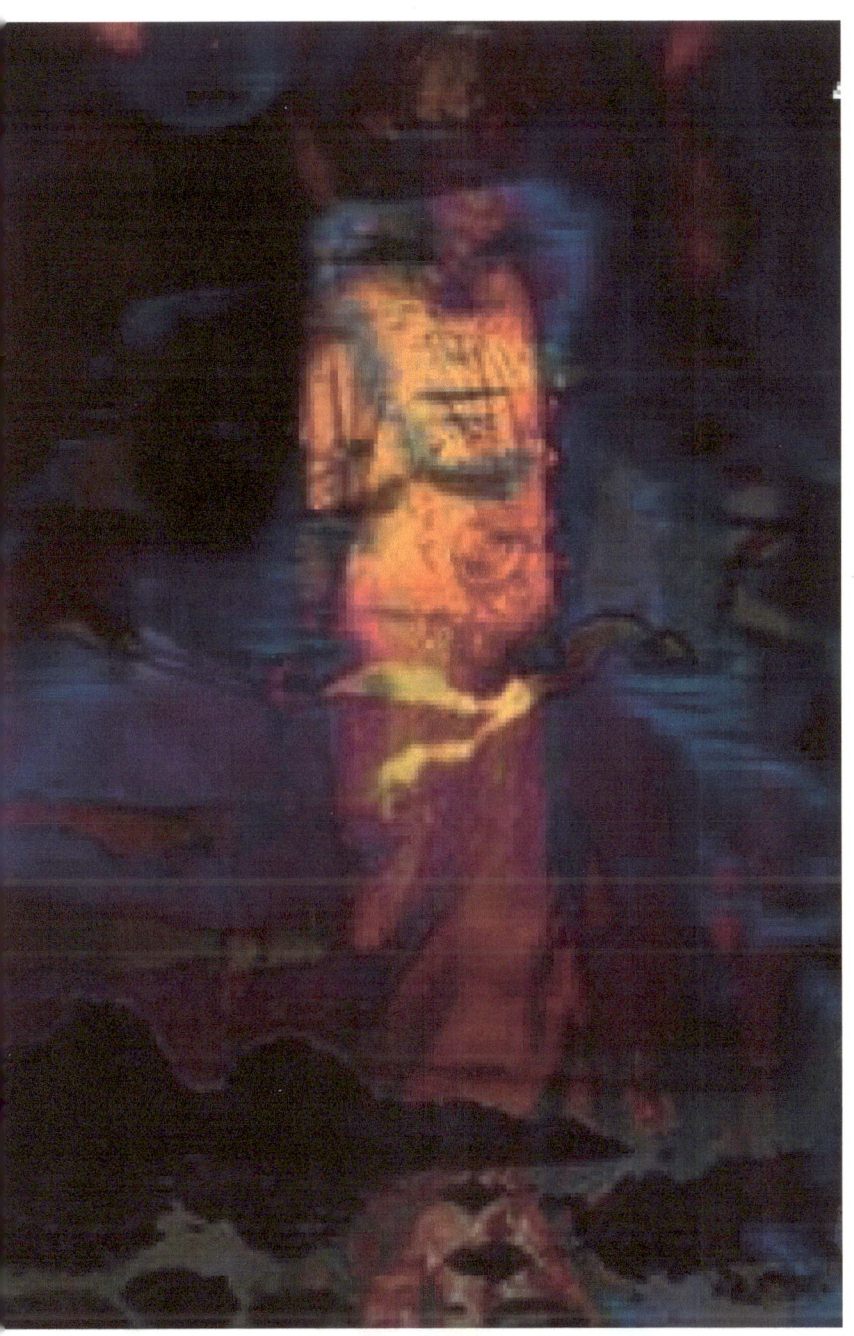

Reflections

Cathleen Jo Faruque ©

Water
Is a timeless
Span
Of never
Ending
Moments.
The infinity
We seek
Is lost

Forever

In the
Ebbing
Tide
Of time.

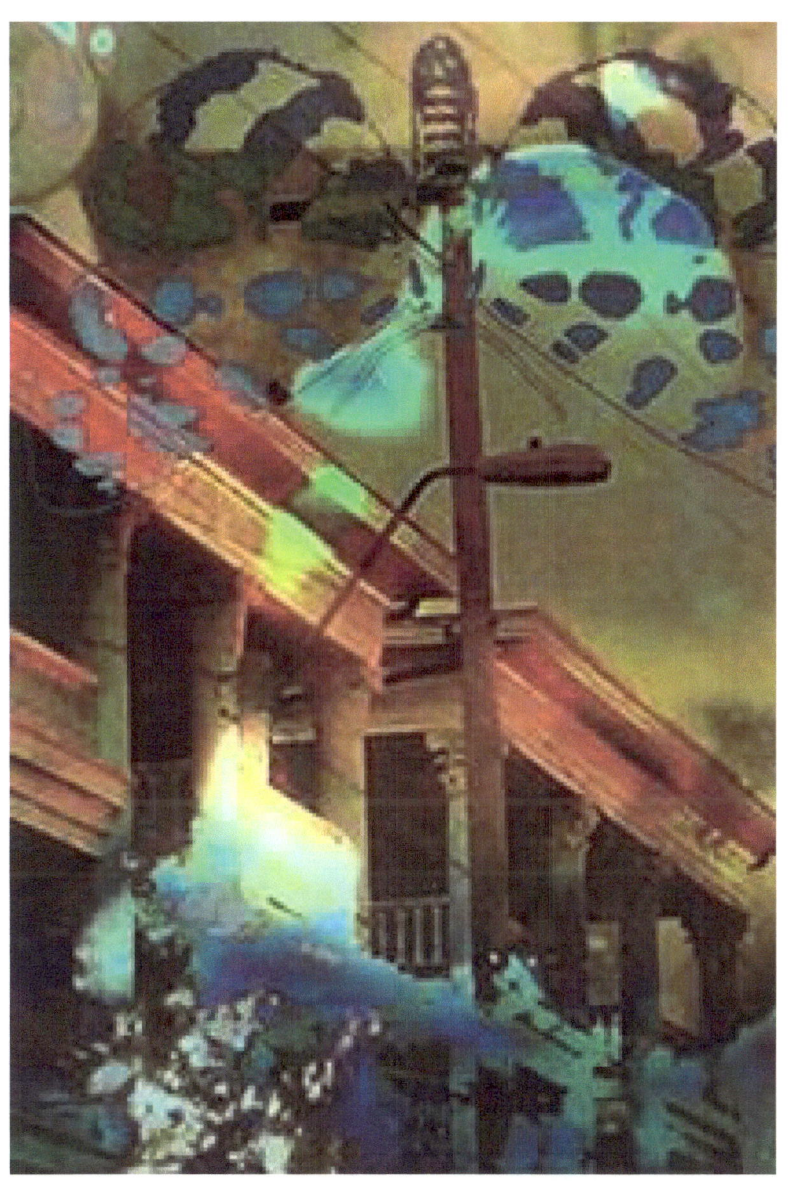

© Amy Folse

Sentiment

Cathleen Jo Faruque ©

Beautiful liquid pools of black
Deeply eternal
Vast as the universe
Embedded in your eyes.
Countless stories
Told through unmoving lips
Endearing tilt gleaming
Bursting form of memories
Forgotten long ago.
Beaming with knowledge of
What was
What is
What will be.
Cast forever in the depth
of beautiful liquid pools of black
deeply eternal
vast as the universe
embedded in your eyes.

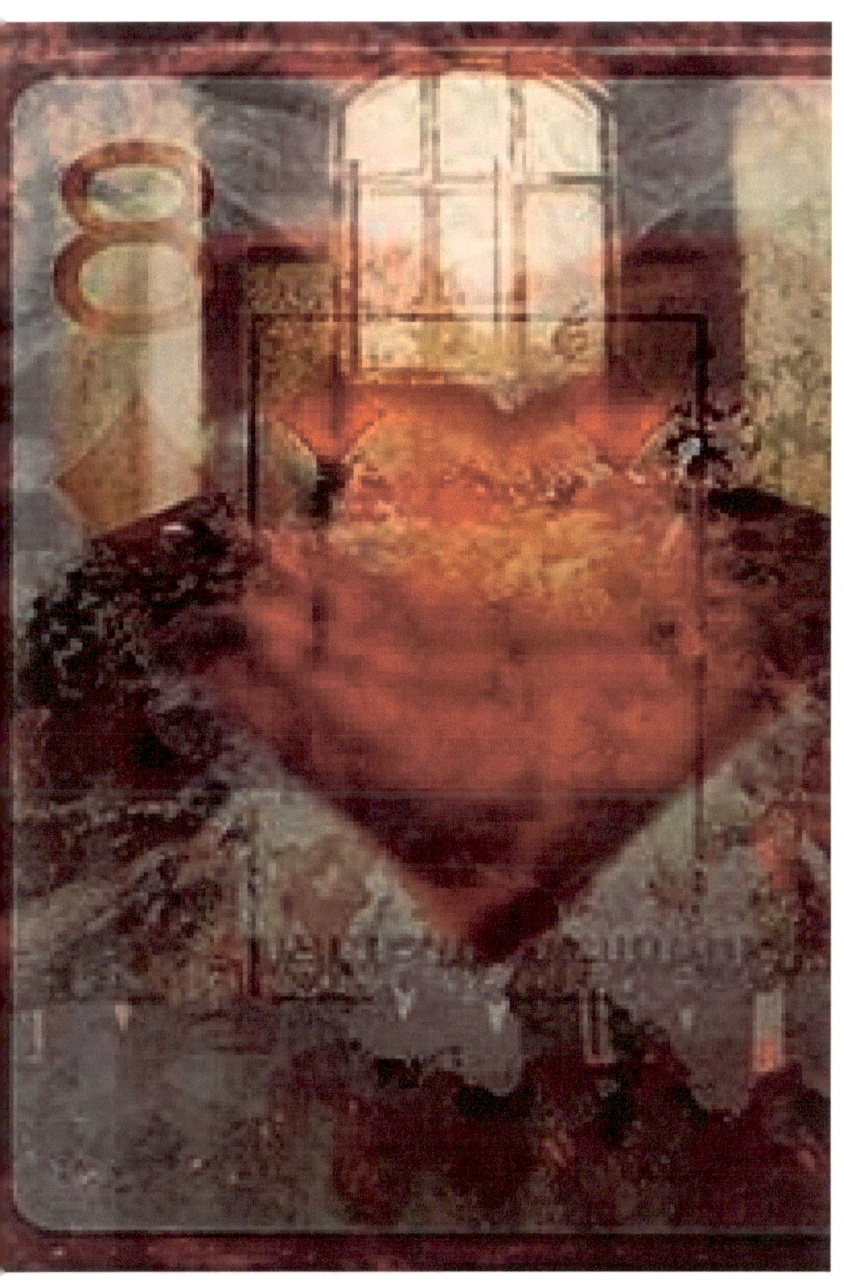

Shadows

Cathleen Jo Faruque ©

As far as Earth's eccentric companion
Distant as the inconstant moon
So are you to me
Space
Time
Distance
Measured in light years
Space is called space
Because there is so much space there
Your heart fills the void
For another
Not me
Energy
Mass
Light
The years passing
Mean nothing to you
Void
Age
Dawn
As the sun embraces
The Earth.

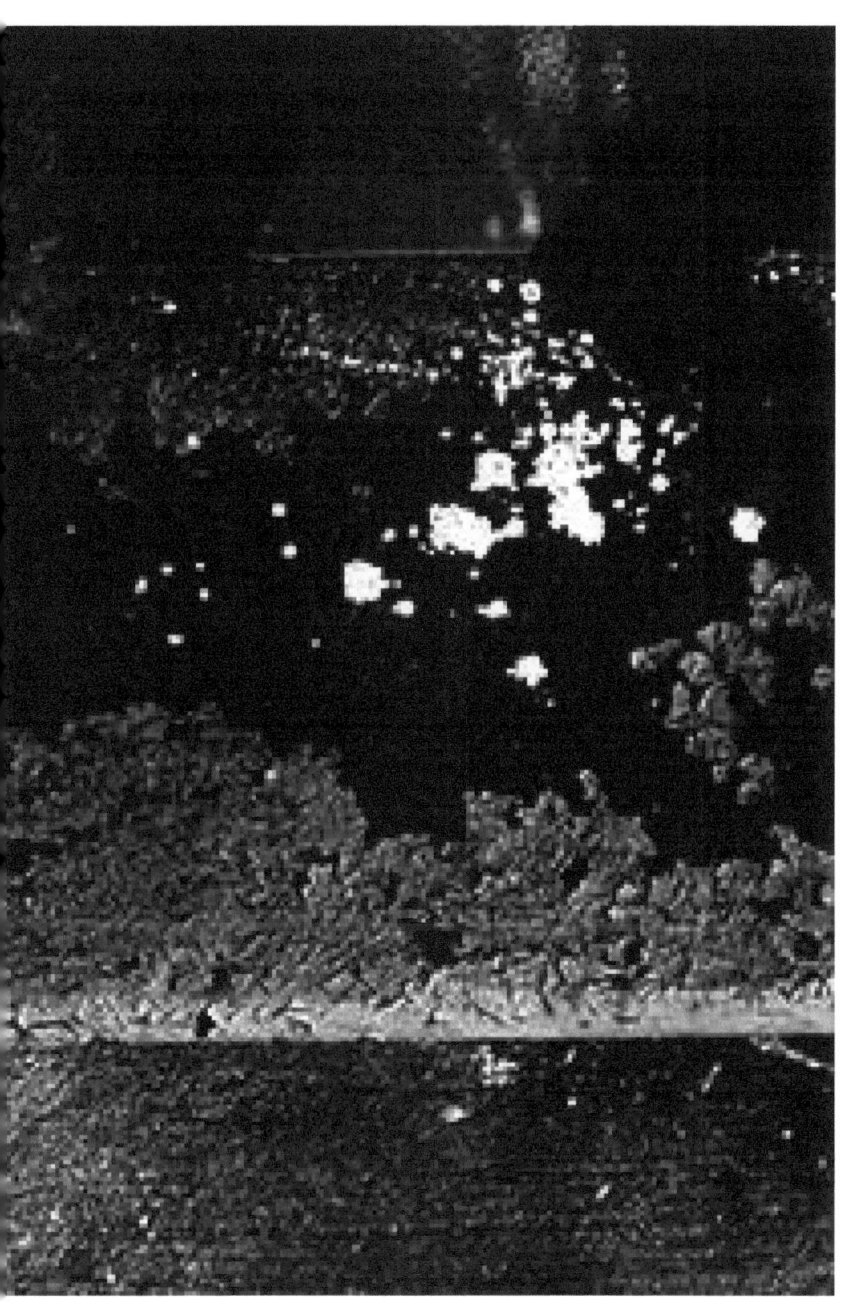

© Amy Folse

Sky Lord

Cathleen Jo Faruque ©

Orion crosses

Shadow moon

Dark hazy blue

Over cloud covered veil

Leafless trees like

Sleeveless Goddesses

Dance to wintery winds.

Moon hangs low

Faceless and careless

A timeless train wreck

Just like you

The disaster I love

To love

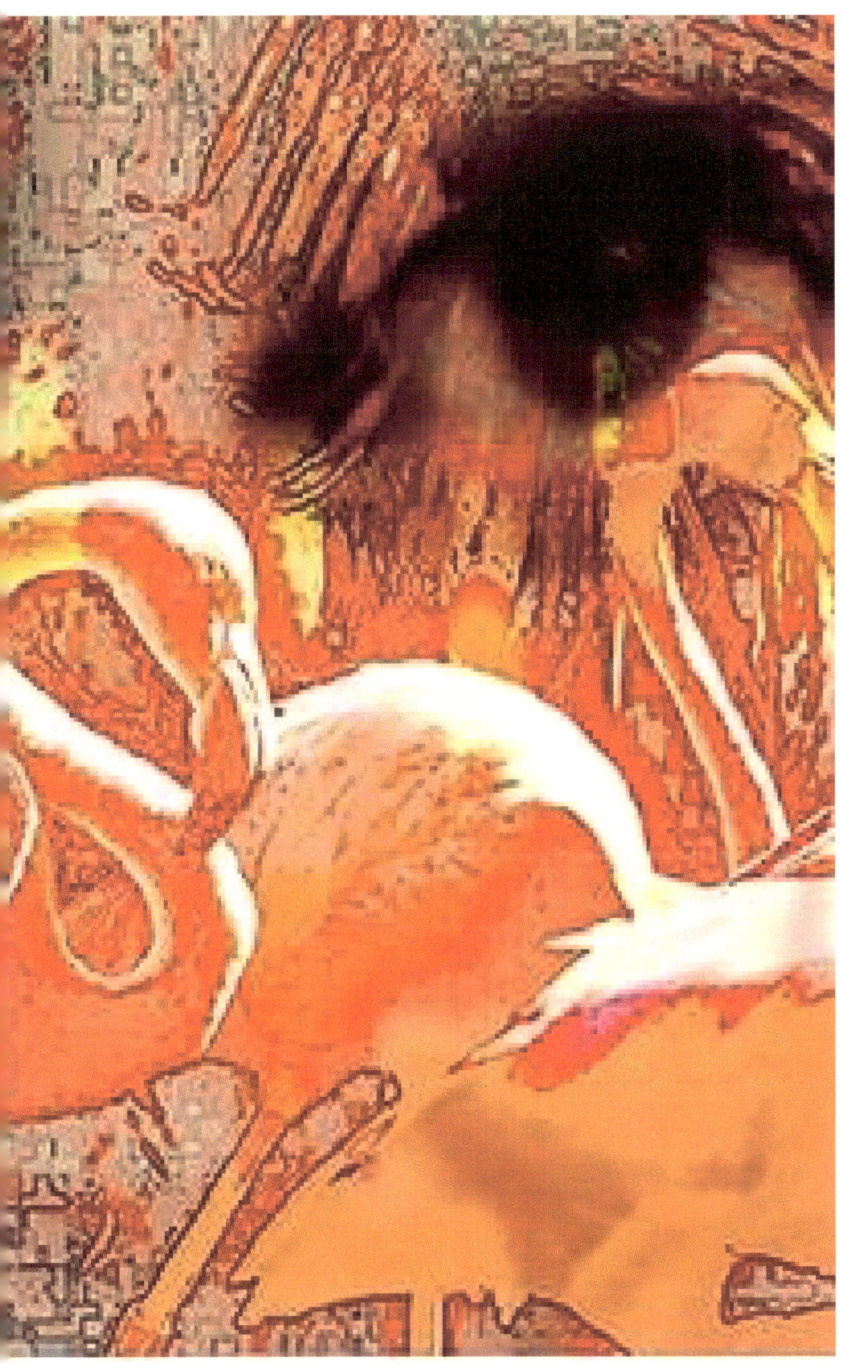

© Amy Folse

Submission

Cathleen Jo Faruque ©

Offer your heart

The cost is too high

Evocative memories

Here comes your ghost again

Stealing through my door

Remind me why I came into

Your arms?

Seasons passed no word from you

Then your voice

Calls my name once again

Like nothing ever happened

Years ago

If you offer me your heart

The cost is too high

Your voice is evocative

It comes back all too clearly

How I loved you dearly

And for this I already paid

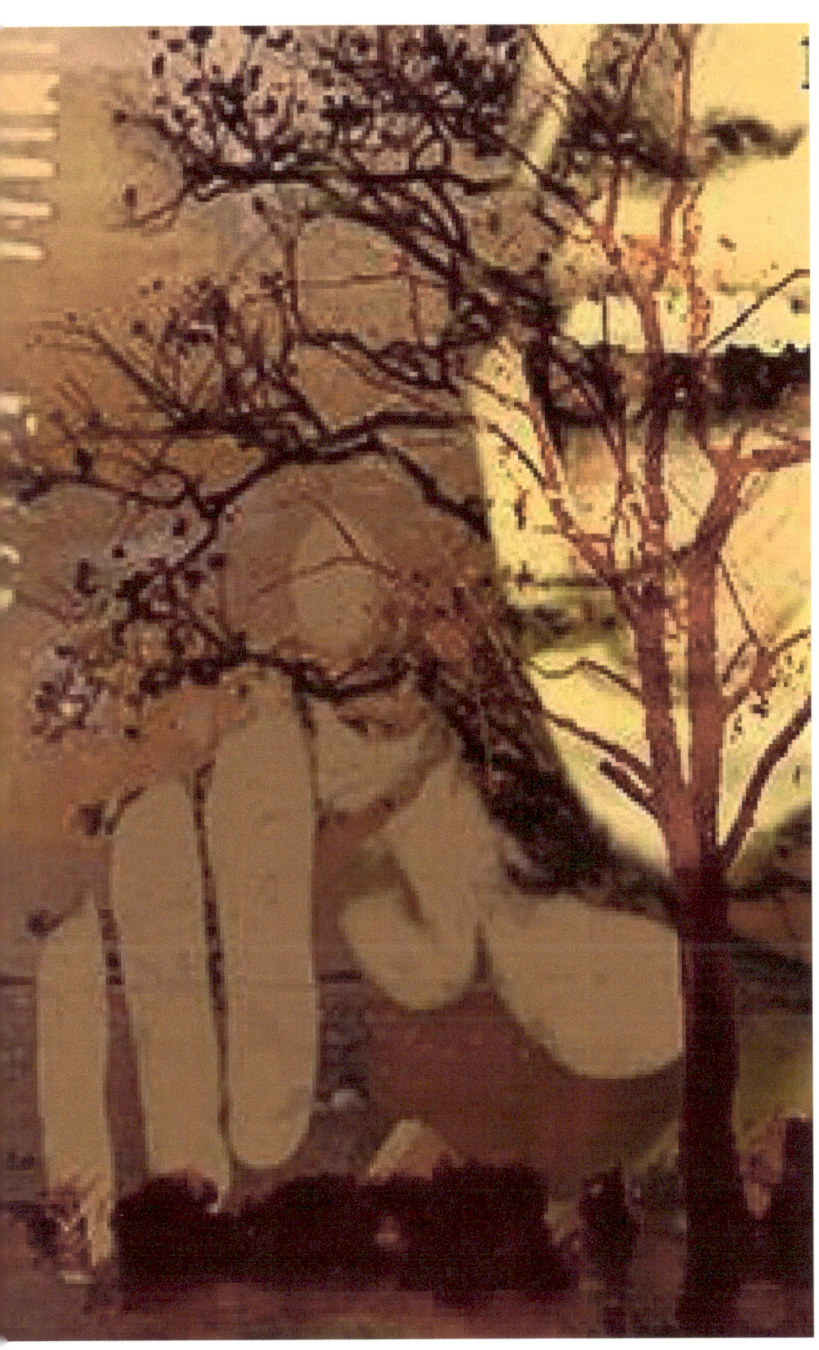

© Amy Folse

The Chasm of Faith

Cathleen Jo Faruque ©

I don't have a handle on you

I believe you are a conspirator

A rogue and a charlatan

Maybe it is my contaminated wits

Maybe it is my covetous heart

Maybe it is my wariness of idiom

But more likely

It is you

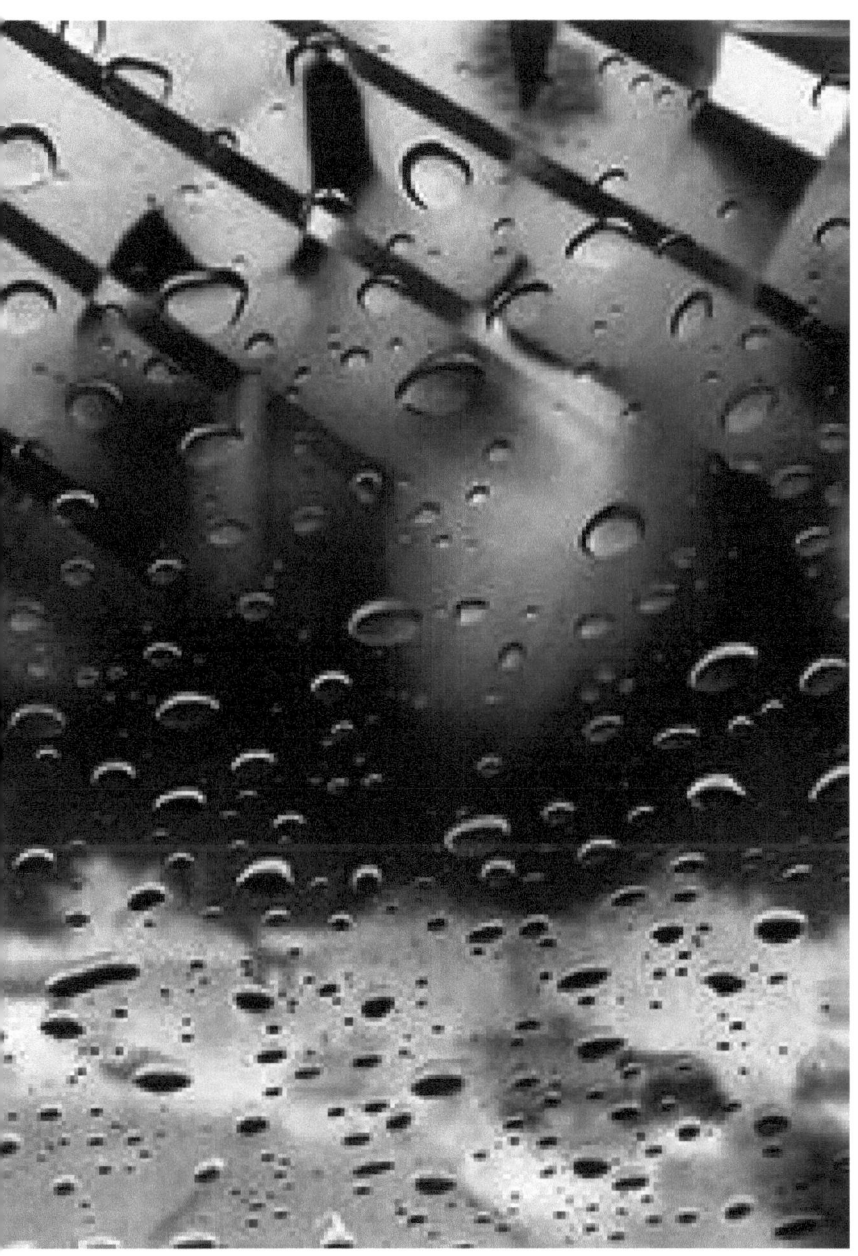

© Amy Folse

The Moon's Embrace

Cathleen Jo Faruque ©

Softly the
Swirl of dark curls
Unfurl
As jet black ink
Pools of expansive
Meaningful depths
Watchfully wait.
Understood through
Conceding look
Presumptuous nod.
Perpetually on edge.
Reflective astral passion
Searching love's embrace
Upon star gazing brow.
Languished distress
For lack of a declaration.
Notable are the differences
Moment in time and space
Absolute to a
Transitory age
Ageless and infinite sphere.
Not a chance
You and I
For only a
Connection
In carefree and
Harmonious
Agony.

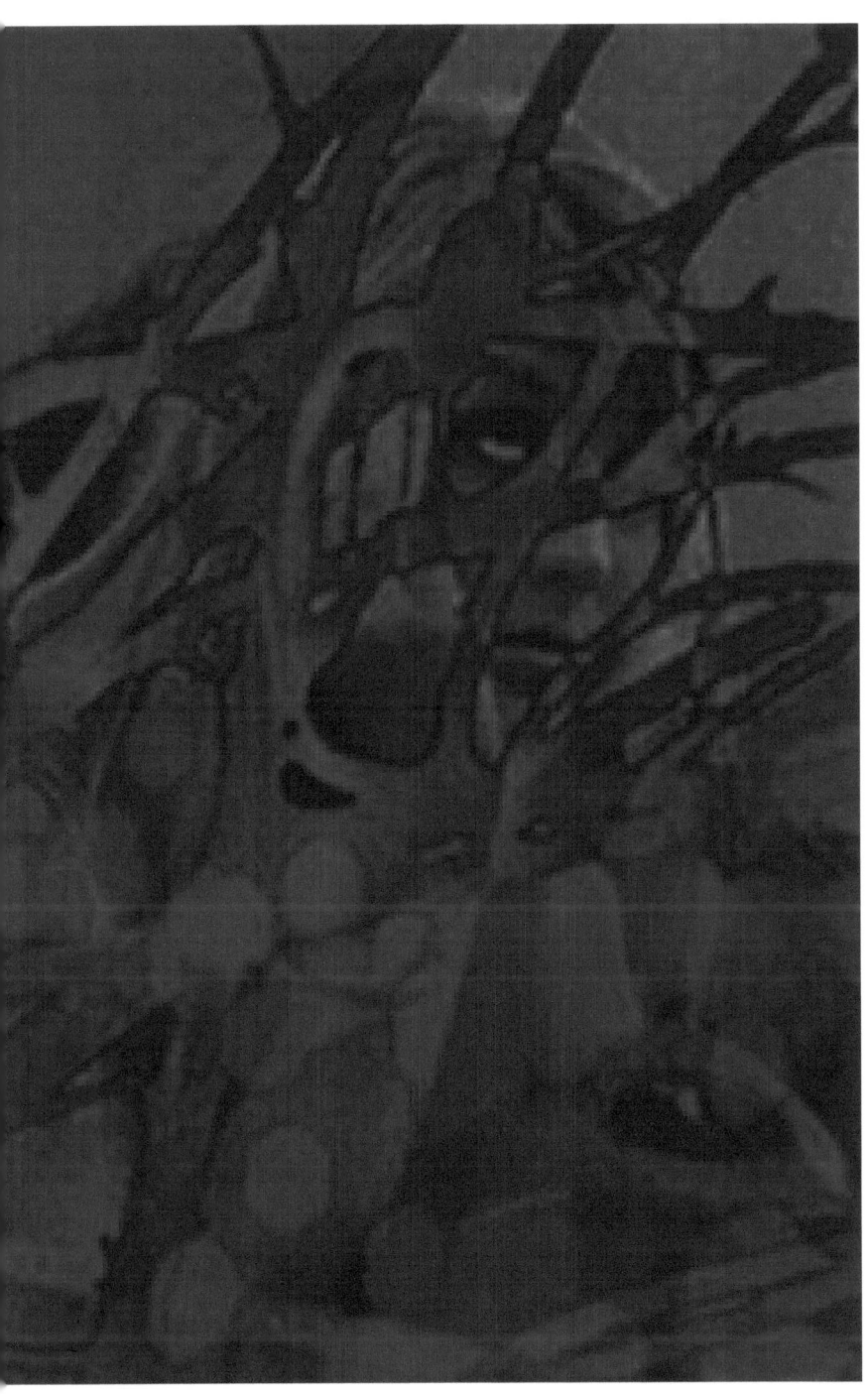

© Amy Folse

The Tear

Cathleen Jo Faruque ©

Drops
Softly
Down
The soft
Pink
Cheek.
Followed by
Another
In the hollows
Blue
Mass
Of tissue.
Gently
It falls
Until it
Hits the
Lips
Salty
Taste
Caress
Flesh
Until it
Encompasses
A world
Of uncaring
Loneliness.

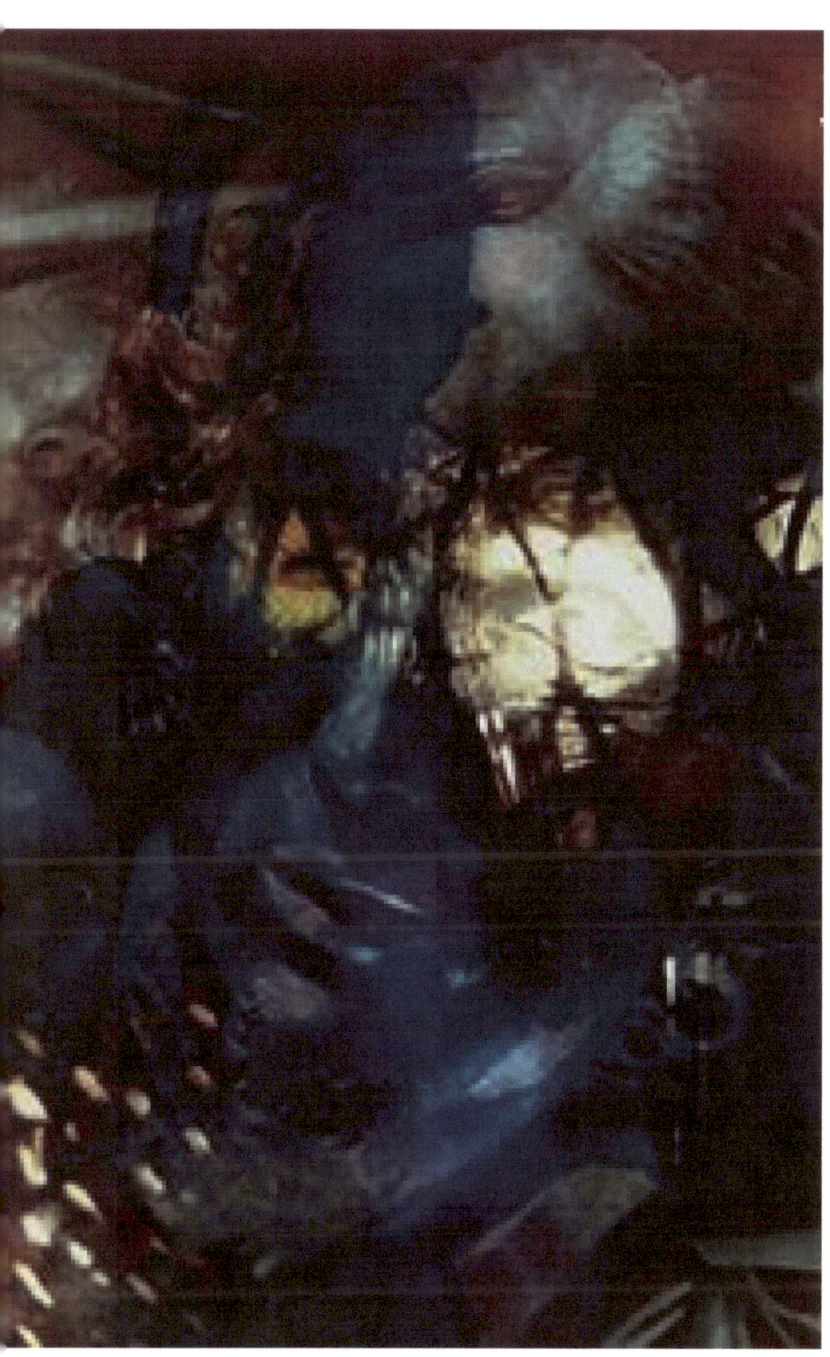

Transitions

Cathleen Jo Faruque ©

Traces
Spaces
Adjusting
Cases,
Uncaring
Faces.

Wondering
Wandering
Meandering
Misleading
Carefree
Crossing.

Lost
At what
Cost.
Pain
Less
Gain
Going
Insane.

Mind
Games
Played
Waltzing
Strayed
Crossings
Laid.

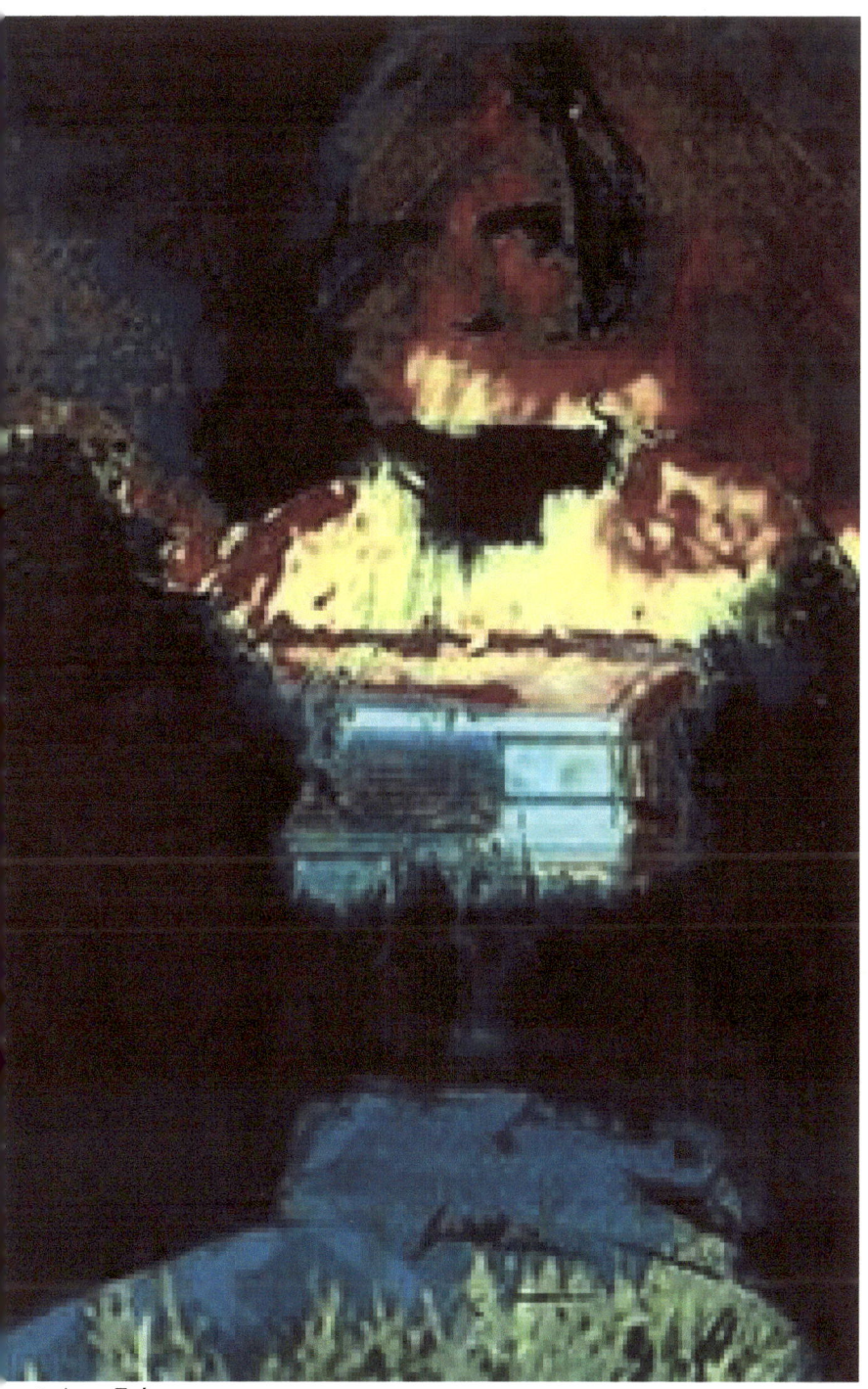

Venial Sins

Cathleen Jo Faruque ©

Does righteousness supersede?

Deception?

At what moment of measure

Does propaganda

Become so insufferable

As to forestall consideration

To human essence?

Should one prolong?

Prevailing,

Allowing the ruse

to rankle, putrefy, and infect

the very core of one's

Existence?

Does one presume veracity?

For the sake of dedication?

At what detriment

To human character?

Absolutes

Elusive procession

Permeate right

Versus iniquitous

Unknown.

Each to their own.

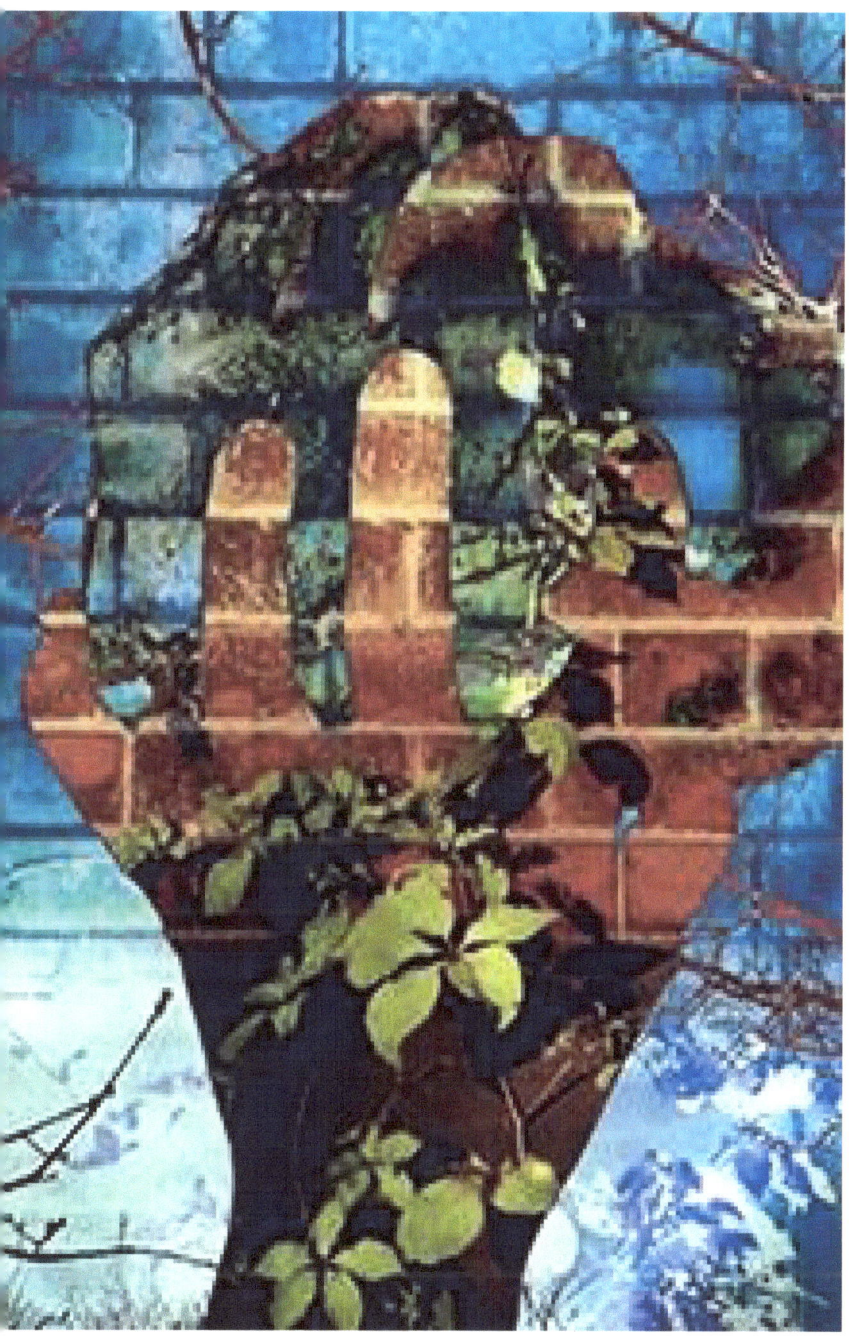

© Amy Folse

Victim

Cathleen Jo Faruque ©

Mystified reflections
Time is a thief
And I am her victim
Night eludes me
Hallucinations scamper
In silence
Reminiscence of remorse
Riposte don't come near
Uncertainty
Resolution
Reservation
Fading veracity
The web of mendacity
Time is a thief
And I am her casualty

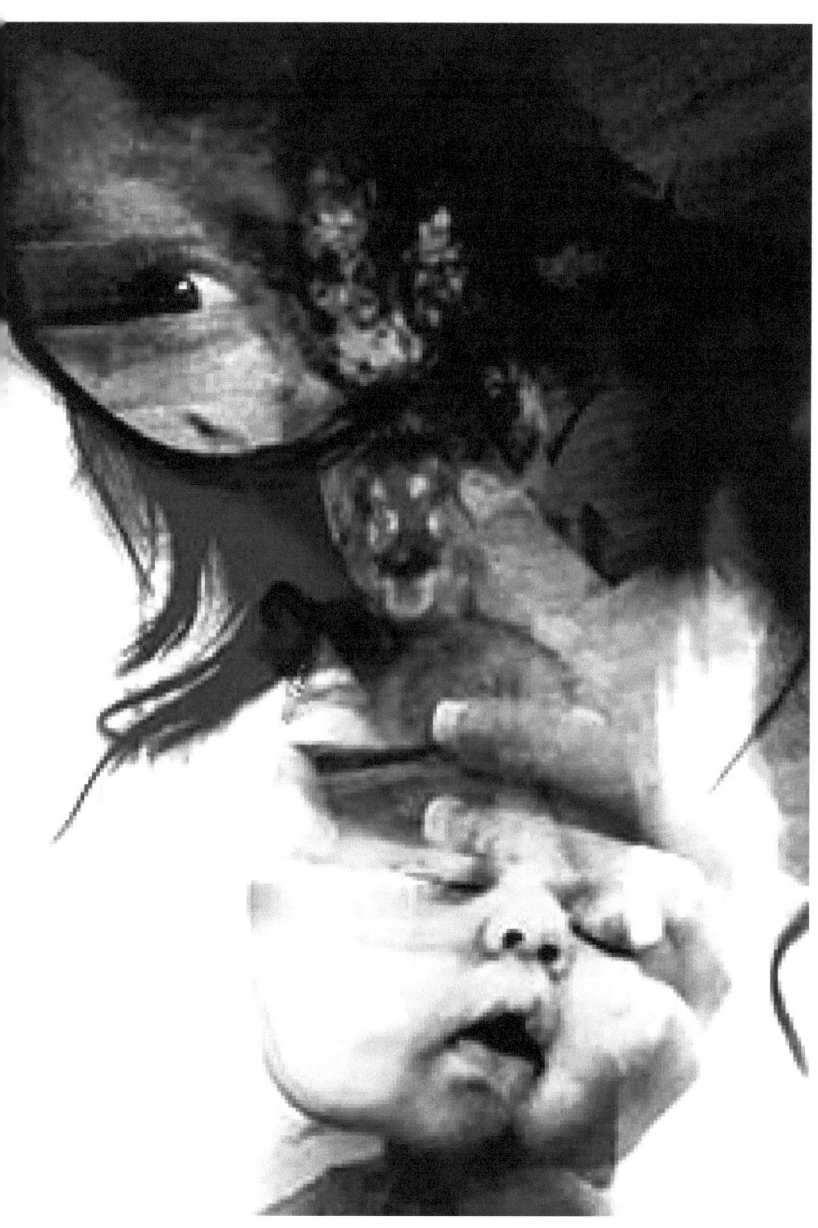

Amy Folse

Wakeful Sleep

Cathleen Jo Faruque ©

Taunt me with your smile
Tease me with your laugh
Coax me with your eyes
Catch me with your heart.
Foolishly caught in the
great web of
time.
Catching me like the
North West winds that
throw wicked waves
on the water's edge.
What a tangle
what a torment.
Why bring out
what was peacefully sleeping
to succumb to desire
never quenched,
Like a thirst never
satisfied
As the ripples of
memory
entice me ever
farther and nearer
to you.

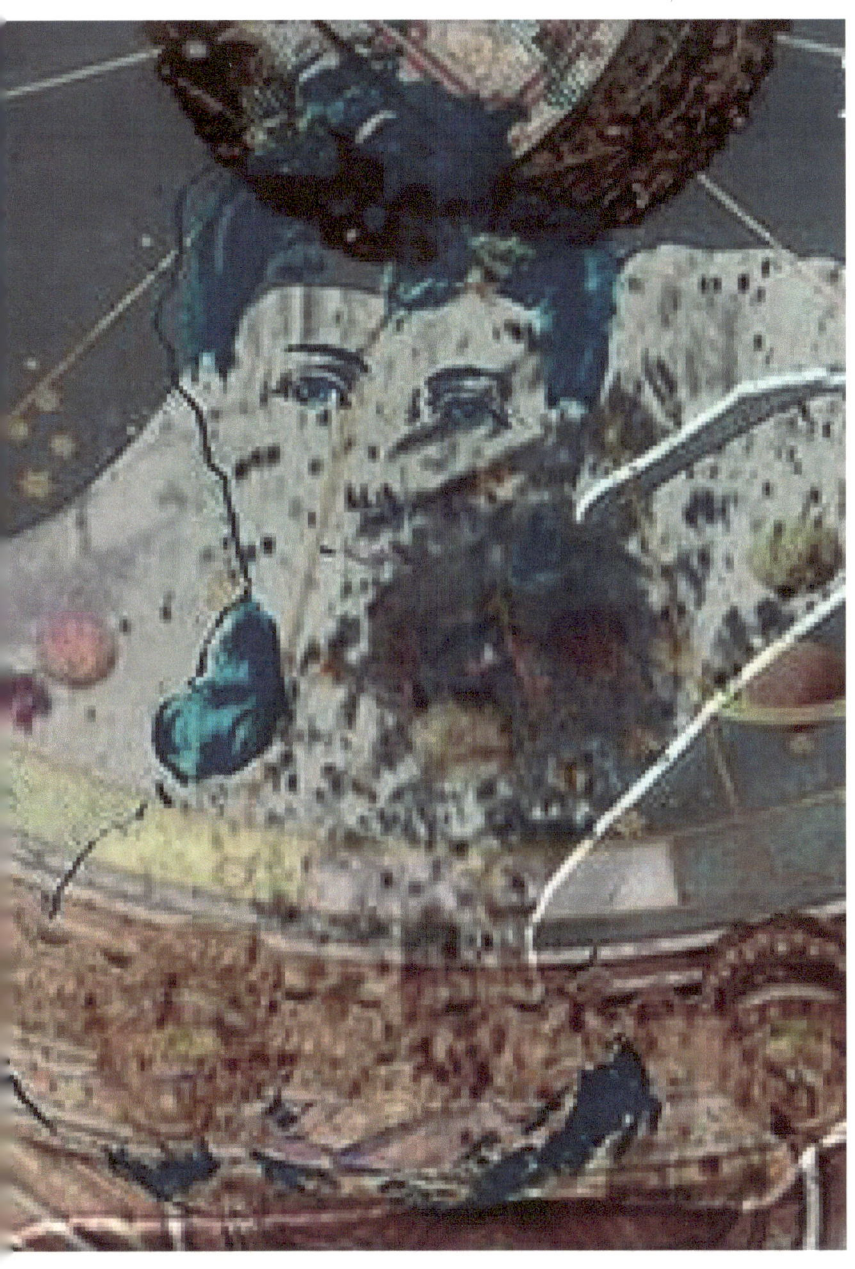

© Amy Folse

Wasted on Youth

Cathleen Jo Faruque ©

A thousand tears
Cast off
For you
Cannot obliterate the
Cynical experience of
The final kiss.
A thousand memories
Withered
For you
Cannot detach from
That conclusive touch
Unsentimental heart
Shattered dreams
Part
Garish pools
Expeditious tides
Of misfortunate
Circumstance
Obscured by
Time.
A thousand thoughts
Reminiscent of you
For love's
Forsaken fruit
Never spoken
Veracity gone astray
No longer an option.

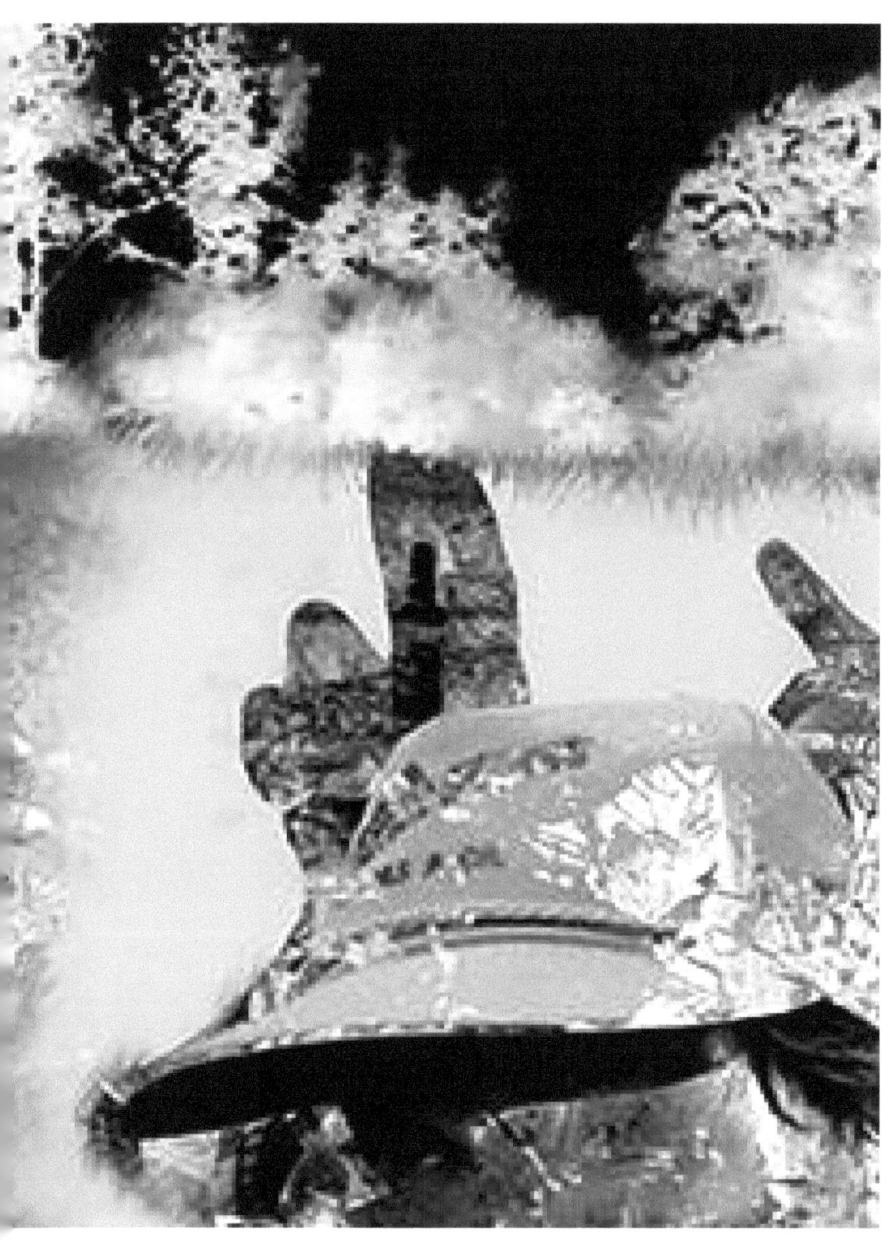

www.ingramcontent.com/pod-product-compliance
Lightning Source LLC
Chambersburg PA
CBHW040844180526
45159CB00001B/307